NOTES ON A NERVOUS PLANET

ALSO BY MATT HAIG

The Last Family in England
The Dead Fathers Club
The Possession of Mr Cave
The Radleys
The Humans
Humans: An A–Z
Reasons to Stay Alive
How to Stop Time

NOTES ON A NERVOUS PLANET

Matt Haig

CANONGATE

Published in Great Britain in 2018 by Canongate Books Ltd,
14 High Street, Edinburgh EH1 1TE

canongate.co.uk

1

British Library Cataloguing-in-Publication Data
A catalogue record for this book is available
on request from the British Library

ISBN 978 1 78689 267 6

Typeset in Granjon 12.5 by Biblichor Ltd, Edinburgh

Printed and bound in Great Britain by Clays Ltd, St Ives plc.

For Andrea

Contents

1   A stressed-out mind in a stressed-out world   1
2   The big picture   35
3   A feeling is not your face   53
4   Notes on time   67
5   Life overload   79
6   Internet anxieties   89
7   Shock of the news   123
8   A small section on sleep   137
9   Priorities   147
10 Phone fears   155
11 The detective of despair   173
12 The thinking body   199
13 The end of reality   211
14 Wanting   221
15 Two lists about work   241
16 Shaping the future   249
17 The song of you   263
18 Everything you are is enough   283

People I'd like to thank   309

'Toto, I've a feeling we're not in Kansas anymore.'

—Dorothy in *The Wizard of Oz*

I

A STRESSED-OUT MIND
IN A STRESSED-OUT WORLD

A conversation, about a year ago

I WAS STRESSED out.

I was walking around in circles, trying to win an argument on the internet. And Andrea was looking at me. Or I *think* Andrea was looking at me. It was hard to tell, as I was looking at my phone.

'Matt? Matt?'

'Uh. Yeah?'

'What's up?' she asked, in the kind of despairing voice that develops with marriage. Or marriage to me.

'Nothing.'

'You haven't looked up from your phone in over an hour. You're just walking around, banging into furniture.'

My heart was racing. There was a tightness in my chest. Fight or flight. I felt cornered and threatened by someone on the internet who lived over 8,000 miles away from me and who I would never meet, but who was still managing to ruin my weekend. 'I'm just getting back to something.'

'Matt, get off there.'

'I just—'

The thing with me... [text obscured by folded corner] that make you feel better in [the] [...] is that so many things worse in the long term. You distrac[...] [...] make you feel you really need is to *know* yourself. [...] what

'Matt!'

An hour later, in the car, Andrea glanced at me in [the] passenger seat. I wasn't on my phone, but I had a tight hold of it, for security, like a nun clutching her rosary.

'Matt, are you okay?'

'Yeah. Why?'

'You look lost. You look like you used to look, when . . .'

She stopped herself saying 'when you had depression' but I knew what she meant. And besides, I could feel anxiety and depression around me. Not actually *there* but close. The memory of it something I could almost touch in the stifling air of the car.

'I'm fine,' I lied. 'I'm fine, I'm fine . . .'

Within a week I was lying on my sofa, falling into my eleventh bout of anxiety.

A life edit

I WAS SCARED. I couldn't not be. Being scared is what anxiety is all about.

The bouts were becoming closer and closer. I was worried where I was heading. It seemed there was no upper limit to despair.

I tried to distract myself out of it. However, I knew from past experience alcohol was off limits. So I did the things that had helped before to climb out of a hole. The things I forget to do in day-to-day life. I was careful about what I ate. I did yoga. I tried to meditate. I lay on the floor and placed my hand on my stomach and inhaled deeply – in, out, in, out – and noticed the stuttery rhythm of my breath.

But everything was difficult. Even choosing what to wear in the morning could make me cry. It didn't matter that I had felt like this before. A sore throat doesn't become less sore simply because you've felt it before.

I tried to read, but found it hard to concentrate.

I listened to podcasts.

I watched new Netflix shows.

I went on social media.

I tried to get on top of my work by replying to all my emails.

I woke up and clasped my phone, and prayed that whatever I could find there could take me out of myself.

But – spoiler alert – it didn't work.

I began to feel worse. And many of the 'distractions' were doing nothing but driving me further to distraction. In T.S. Eliot's phrase from his *Four Quartets*, I was 'distracted from distraction by distraction'.

I would stare at an unanswered email, with a feeling of dread, and not be able to answer it. Then, on Twitter, my go-to digital distraction of choice, I noticed my anxiety intensify. Even just passively scrolling my timeline felt like an exposure of a wound.

I read news websites – another distraction – and my mind couldn't take it. The knowledge of so much suffering in the world didn't help put my pain in perspective. It just made me feel powerless. And pathetic that my invisible woes were so paralysing when there were so many *visible* woes in the world. My despair intensified.

So I decided to do something.

I disconnected.

I chose not to look at social media for a few days. I put an auto-response on my emails, too. I stopped watching or reading the news. I didn't watch TV. I didn't watch any music videos. Even magazines I avoided. (During my initial breakdown, years before, the bright imagery of magazines always used to linger and clog my mind with feverish racing images as I tried to sleep.)

I left my phone downstairs when I went to bed. I tried to get outside more. My bedside table was cluttered with a chaos of wires and technology and books I wasn't really reading. So I tidied up and took them away, too.

In the house, I tried to lie in darkness as much as possible, the way you might deal with a migraine. I had always, since I was first suicidally ill in my twenties, understood that getting better involved a kind of life edit.

A *taking away*.

As the minimalism advocate Fumio Sasaki puts it: 'there's a happiness in having less'. In the early days of my first experience of panic the only things I had taken away were booze and cigarettes and strong coffees. Now, though, years later, I realised that a more general overload was the problem.

A life overload.

And certainly a technology overload. The only real

technology I interacted with during this present recovery – aside from the car and the cooker – were yoga videos on YouTube, which I watched with the brightness turned low.

The anxiety didn't miraculously disappear. Of course not.

Unlike my smartphone, there is no 'slide to power off' function for anxiety.

But I stopped *feeling worse*. I plateaued. And after a few days, things began to calm.

The familiar path of recovery arrived sooner rather than later. And abstaining from stimulants – not just alcohol and caffeine, but these other things – was part of the process.

I began, in short, to feel free again.

How this book came about

MOST PEOPLE KNOW the modern world can have physical effects. That, despite advances, aspects of modern life are dangerous for our bodies. Car accidents, smoking, air pollution, a sofa-dwelling lifestyle, takeaway pizza, radiation, that fourth glass of Merlot.

Even being at a laptop can pose physical dangers. Sitting down all day, getting an RSI. Once I was even told by an optician that my eye infection and blocked tear ducts were caused by staring at a screen. We blink less, apparently, when working on a computer.

So, as physical health and mental health are intertwined, couldn't the same be said about the modern world and our mental states? Couldn't aspects of how we live in the modern world be responsible for how we *feel* in the modern world?

Not just in terms of the *stuff* of modern life, but its values, too. The values that cause us to want more than we have. To worship work above play. To compare the worst bits of ourselves with the best bits of other people. To feel like we always *lack* something.

And as I grew better, by the day, I began to have an idea about a book – this book right here.

I had already written about my mental health in *Reasons to Stay Alive*. But the question now was not: *why should I stay alive?* The question this time was a broader one: *how can we live in a mad world without ourselves going mad?*

News from a nervous planet

AS I BEGAN researching I quickly found some attention-grabbing headlines for an attention-grabbing age. Of course, news is almost *designed* to stress us out. If it was designed to keep us calm it wouldn't be news. It would be yoga. Or a puppy. So there is an irony about news companies reporting on anxiety while also making us anxious.

Anyway, here are some of those headlines:

STRESS AND SOCIAL MEDIA FUEL MENTAL HEALTH CRISIS AMONG GIRLS (*The Guardian*)

CHRONIC LONELINESS IS A MODERN-DAY EPIDEMIC (*Forbes*)

FACEBOOK 'MAY MAKE YOU MISERABLE', SAYS FACEBOOK (*Sky News*)

'STEEP RISE' IN SELF-HARM AMONG TEENAGERS (BBC)

WORKPLACE STRESS AFFECTS 73 PER CENT OF EMPLOYEES (*The Australian*)

STARK RISE IN EATING DISORDERS BLAMED ON OVER-EXPOSURE TO CELEBRITIES' BODIES (*The Guardian*)

SUICIDE ON CAMPUS AND THE PRESSURE OF PERFECTION (*The New York Times*)

WORKPLACE STRESS RISING SHARPLY (*Radio New Zealand*)

WILL ROBOTS TAKE OUR CHILDREN'S JOBS? (*The New York Times*)

STRESS, HOSTILITY RISING IN AMERICAN HIGH SCHOOLS IN TRUMP ERA (*The Washington Post*)

CHILDREN IN HONG KONG ARE RAISED TO EXCEL, NOT TO BE HAPPY (*South China Morning Post*)

HIGH ANXIETY: MORE AND MORE PEOPLE ARE TODAY TURNING TO DRUGS TO DEAL WITH STRESS (*El País*)

ARMY OF THERAPISTS TO BE SENT INTO SCHOOLS TO TACKLE ANXIETY EPIDEMIC (*The Telegraph*)

IS THE INTERNET GIVING US ALL ADHD? (*The Washington Post*)

'OUR MINDS CAN BE HIJACKED': THE TECH INSIDERS WHO FEAR A SMARTPHONE DYSTOPIA (*The Guardian*)

TEENAGERS ARE GROWING MORE ANXIOUS AND DEPRESSED
(The Economist)

INSTAGRAM WORST SOCIAL MEDIA APP FOR YOUNG PEOPLE'S MENTAL HEALTH (CNN)

WHY ARE RATES OF SUICIDE SOARING ACROSS THE PLANET? (Alternet)

As I said, it is ironic that reading the news about how things are making us anxious and depressed actually can make us anxious, and that tells us as much as the headlines themselves.

The aim in this book isn't to say that everything is a disaster and we're all screwed, because we already have Twitter for that. No. The aim isn't even to say that the modern world has uniformly worse problems than before. In some specific ways it is getting measurably better. In figures from the World Bank, the number of people world-wide living in severe economic hardship is falling radically, with over one billion people moving out of extreme poverty in the last thirty years. And think of all the millions of children's lives around the globe saved by vaccinations. As Nicholas Kristof pointed out in a 2017 *New York Times* article, 'if just about the worst thing that can happen is for a parent to lose a child, that's about half as likely as it was in 1990.' So for all the ongoing violence and intolerance and economic injustice prevalent in our species, there are – on the most global of scales – also reasons for pride and hope.

The problem is that each age poses a unique and complex set of challenges. And while many things have improved, not all things have. Inequalities still remain. And some new problems have arisen. People often live in fear, or feel inadequate, or even suicidal, when they have – materially – more than ever.

And I am keenly aware that the oft-used approach of pointing out a list of advantages of modern life, such as health and education and average income, does not help. It is like a wagging finger telling a depressed person to count her blessings because no one has died. This book seeks to recognise that what we feel is just as important as what we have. That mental wellbeing counts as much as physical wellbeing – indeed, that it is part of physical wellbeing. And that, on these terms, something is going wrong.

If the modern world is making us feel bad, then it doesn't matter what else we have going for us, because feeling bad sucks. And feeling bad when we are told there is no reason to, well, that sucks even more.

I want this book to put these stressed-out headlines in context, and to look at how to protect ourselves in a world of potential panic. Because, whatever else we have going for ourselves, our minds are still vulnerable. Many mental health problems are quantifiably rising, and – if we believe our mental wellbeing is important – we need, quite desperately, to look at what might be behind these changes.

Mental health problems are not:

A bandwagon.

Fashionable.

A fad.

A celebrity trend.

A result of a growing awareness of mental health problems.

Always easy to talk about.

The same as they always were.

Yin to the yang

SO, IT IS a tale of two realities.

Many of us, it is true, have a lot to be grateful for in the developed world. The rise in life expectancy, the decline in infant mortality, the availability of food and shelter, the absence of major all-encompassing world wars. We have addressed many of our basic physical needs. So many of us live in relative day-to-day safety, with roofs over our heads and food on the table. But after solving some problems, are we left with others? Have some social advances brought new problems? Of course.

It sometimes feels as if we have temporarily solved the problem of scarcity and replaced it with the problem of excess.

Everywhere we look, people are seeking ways to change their lifestyles, by taking things away. Diets are the obvious example of this passion for restriction, but think also of the trend for dedicating whole months in the calendar to veganism or sobriety, and the growing desire for 'digital detoxes'. The growth in mindfulness, meditation and minimal living is a visible response to an overloaded culture. A yin to the frantic yang of 21st-century life.

Breakdown

AS I LEFT my most recent bout of anxiety behind me, I began to waver.

Maybe this was all a stupid idea.

I began to wonder if it was a bad thing to dwell on *problems*. But then I remembered that it is precisely *not* talking about problems that is itself a problem. It's what causes people to break down in their office or classroom. It's what fills up addiction units and hospitals and raises suicide figures. And in the end I decided that, for me, knowing this stuff is essential. I want to find reasons to be positive, and ways to be happy, but first you need to know the reality of the situation.

For instance, personally I need to know why I have a fear of *slowing down*, like I am the bus in *Speed* that would explode if it dropped below 50 miles per hour. I want to work out if the speed of me relates to the speed of the world.

The reason is simple, and partly selfish. I am petrified of where my mind can go, because I know where it has already been. And I also know that part of the reason I became ill in my twenties was to do with the way I was living. Hard drinking, bad sleeping, aspiring to be something I wasn't, and the pressures of society at large. I never want to fall back into that place, and so I need to be alert not only to where stress can take people, but also where it comes from. I want to know if one of the reasons I sometimes feel like I am on the brink of a breakdown is partly because the world sometimes seems on the brink of a breakdown.

Breakdown is an unspecific word, which might explain why medical professionals shy away from it these days, but at its root we understand what it conveys. The dictionary defines it as '1. A mechanical failure' and '2. A failure of a relationship or system'.

And it doesn't take too much looking to see the warning signs of a breakdown not just inside our selves, but in the wider world. It might sound dramatic to say the planet could be heading for a breakdown. But we do know beyond doubt that in all kinds of ways – technologically, environmentally, politically – the world is changing. And fast. So we need, more than ever, to know how to edit the world, so it can never break us down.

Life is beautiful (but)

LIFE IS BEAUTIFUL.

Even modern life. Maybe even *especially* modern life. We are saturated with a billion kinds of transient magic. We can pick up a device and contact people a whole hemisphere away. We can, when choosing a holiday, look at the reviews of people who stayed in our desired hotel last week. We can look at satellite images of every road in Timbuktu. When we are ill, we can go to the doctor and get antibiotics for illnesses that could once have killed us. We can go to a supermarket and buy dragon fruit from Vietnam and wine from Chile. If a politician says or does something we disagree with, it has never been easier to voice that disagreement. We can access more information, more films, more books, more *everything*, than ever before.

When, back in the 1990s, Microsoft's slogan asked, 'Where do you want to go today?' it was a rhetorical question. In the digital age, the answer is *everywhere*. Anxiety, to quote the philosopher Søren Kierkegaard, may be the 'dizziness of freedom', but all this freedom of choice really is a miracle.

But while choice is infinite, our lives have time spans. We can't live every life. We can't watch every film or read every book or visit every single place on this sweet earth. Rather than being blocked by it, we need to edit the choice in front of us. We need to find out what is good for us, and leave the rest. We don't need another world. Everything we need is here, if we give up thinking we need everything.

Invisible sharks

ONE FRUSTRATION WITH anxiety is that it is often hard to find a reason behind it. There may be no visible threat and yet you can feel utterly terrified. It's all intense suspense, no action. It's like *Jaws* without the shark.

But often there are sharks. Metaphorical, invisible sharks. Because even when we sometimes feel we are worried for no reason, the reasons are there.

'You're gonna need a bigger boat,' said Chief Brody, in *Jaws* itself.

And maybe that's the problem for us, too. Not the metaphorical sharks but our metaphorical boats. Maybe we would cope with the world better if we knew where those sharks were, and what we need to navigate the waters of life unscathed.

Crash

I SOMETIMES FEEL like my head is a computer with too many windows open. Too much clutter on the desktop. There is a metaphorical spinning rainbow wheel inside me. Disabling me. And if only I could find a way to switch off some of the frames, if only I could drag some of the clutter into the trash, then I would be fine. But which frame would I choose, when they all seem so essential? How can I stop my mind being overloaded when the world is overloaded? We can think about *anything*. And so it makes sense that we end up sometimes thinking about *everything*. We might have to, sometimes, be brave enough to switch the screens off in order to switch ourselves back on. To disconnect in order to reconnect.

Things that are faster than they used to be

Mail.
Cars.
Olympic sprinters.
News.
Processing power.
Photographs.
Scenes in movies.
Financial transactions.
Journeys.
World population growth.
The deforestation of the Amazon rainforest.
Navigation.
Technological progress.
Relationships.
Political events.
The thoughts in your head.

24/7 catastrophe

WORRY IS A small, sweet word that sounds like you could keep an eye on it. Yet worry about the future – the next ten minutes, the next ten years – is the chief obstacle I have to being able to live in and appreciate the present moment.

I am a catastrophiser. I don't simply *worry*. No. My worry has real ambition. My worry is limitless. My anxiety – even when I don't have capital-A *Anxiety* – is big enough to go anywhere. I have always found it easy to think of the worst-case scenario and dwell on it.

And I've been like this for as long as I can remember. I have gone to the doctor many times, convinced of my imminent demise because of an illness I've googled myself into having. As a child, if my mum was late picking me up from primary school it would only take about a minute for me to convince myself she had probably died in a hideous car accident. That never happened, but it's continual not-happening-ness never stopped the possibility that it *could* happen. Every moment my mother wasn't there was a moment in which she might *never* be there again.

The ability to imagine catastrophe in horrific detail, to picture the mangled metal and the spray of white-blue glass glittering on the road, occupied my mind far more than the rational idea that such a catastrophe was unlikely. If Andrea doesn't pick up her phone I can't help but think a likely scenario is that she has fallen down the stairs or maybe even spontaneously combusted. I worry that I upset people without meaning to. I worry that I don't check my privilege enough. I worry about people being in prison for crimes they didn't do. I worry about human rights abuses. I worry about prejudice and politics and pollution and the world my children and their entire generation are inheriting from us. I worry about all the species going extinct because of humans. I worry about my carbon footprint. I worry about all the pain in the world that I am not actively able to stop. I worry about how much I'm wrapped up in myself, which makes me even more wrapped up in myself.

Years before I ever had actual sex I found it easy to imagine I had AIDS, so powerful were the British Government's terrifying public awareness TV slots in the 1980s. If I eat food that tastes a little funny, I immediately imagine I will be hospitalised from food poisoning, even though I have only had food poisoning once in my life.

I can't be at an airport and not feel – and therefore *act* – suspicious.

Every new lump or ulcer or mole is a potential cancer. Every memory lapse is early-onset Alzheimer's. On and on and on. And all this is when I am feeling relatively okay. When I'm ill the catastrophising goes into overdrive.

In fact, now I think about it, that is the chief characteristic of anxiety for me. The continual imagining of how *things could get so much worse*. And it is only recently that I have been understanding how much the world feeds into this. How our mental states – whether we are actually ill or just *stressed out* – are to a degree products of social states. *And vice versa*. I want to understand what it is about this nervous planet that *gets in*.

There is a world of difference between feeling a bit stressed and being properly ill, but as with, say, hunger and starvation, the two are related in that what is bad for one (lack of food) is also bad for the other. And so, when I am well – but stressed – the things that make me feel a little bit worse are often the things that make me feel *much* worse when I am ill. What you learn when you are ill, about what hurts, can then be applied to the better times, too. Pain is one hell of a teacher.

Some more worries on top of those mentioned in the last chapter (because there are always more worries)

– The news.

– Underground trains. When I am on the tube, I imagine all the things that could go wrong. The train could get trapped in the tunnel. There could be a fire. There could be a terrorist incident. I could have a heart attack. To be fair, I once did have a legitimately terrifying experience on an underground train. I stepped off the Paris Métro and into wispy mouth-burning clouds of tear gas. There was a battle going on above ground between union workers and police, and the police had set off some tear gas a bit too close to the Métro station. I didn't know this at the time. At the time, covering my face with a scarf just to breathe, I thought it was a terrorist attack. It wasn't. But simply thinking it was one was a kind of trauma. As Montaigne put it, 'He who fears he shall suffer, already suffers what he fears.'

– Suicide. Although I was suicidal when I was younger, and very nearly threw myself off a cliff, in more recent

times my obsession with suicide became more a fear of doing it, rather than a will to do it.

– *Other health worries*. Such as: sudden and total heart failure from a panic attack (a ludicrously improbable occurrence); a depression so annihilating I wouldn't be able to move ever again and would be stuck there for ever, as though I had gazed on the face of Medusa; cancer; heart disease (I have high cholesterol, for hereditary reasons); dying too young; dying too old; mortality in general.

– *Looks*. It is an outdated myth that men don't worry about their looks. I have worried about my looks. I used to buy *Men's Health* magazine religiously and follow the workouts in an attempt to look like the cover model. I have worried about my hair – the substance of it, the potential loss of it. I used to worry about the moles on my face. I used to stare for long periods in the mirror, as if I could convince it to change its mind. I still worry about the lines on my face, but I am getting better. It might be a strange irony that the cure for worrying about ageing is sometimes, well, *ageing*.

– *Guilt*. At times I have felt the guilt of being a less than perfect son, and husband, and citizen, and human organism. I feel guilt when I work too hard – and neglect my family – and guilt when I don't work hard enough. The guilt doesn't always have a cause, though. Sometimes it is just a feeling.

– *Inadequacy*. I worry about a lack and I worry about how I can fill it. I often sense a metaphorical void inside me that I have at various times in my life tried to fill with all kinds of stuff – alcohol, partying, tweets, prescription drugs, recreational drugs, exercise, food, work, popularity, travel, spending money, earning more money, getting published – that of course haven't fully worked. The things I have thrown in the hole have often just deepened the hole.

– *Nuclear weapons*. If nuclear weapons have been on the news – which seems to happen on increasing amount these days – I can visualise mushroom clouds through every window. The words of former US general Omar Nelson Bradley offer a chilly echo today: 'Ours is a world of nuclear giants and ethical infants. We know more about killing that we know about living.'

– *Robots*. I am only half joking. Our robotic future is a legitimate source of worry. I boycott self-service checkouts in a continual act of pro-human defiance. But the flip side is that thinking about robots sometimes makes me value the tantalising mystery of being alive.

Five reasons to be happy you are a human and not a sentient robot

1. William Shakespeare was not a robot. Emily Dickinson was not a robot. Neither was Aristotle. Or Euclid. Or Picasso. Or Mary Shelley (though she would be writing about them). Everyone you have ever loved and cared for was not a robot. Humans are amazing to other humans. And we are humans.

2. We are mysterious. We don't know why we are here. We have to craft our own meaning. A robot is designed for tasks or a set of tasks. We have been here for thousands of generations and we are still seeking answers. The mystery is tantalising.

3. Your not-so-distant ancestors wrote poems and acted courageously in wars and fell in love and danced and gazed wistfully at sunsets. A future sentient robot's ancestors will be a self-service checkout and a faulty vacuum cleaner.

4. This list actually has only four things. Just to confuse the robots. Though I did ask some online friends why

humans are better than robots, and they said all kinds of stuff: 'self-deprecating humour', 'love', 'soft skin and orgasms', 'wonder', 'empathy'. And maybe a robot could one day develop these things, but right now it is a good reminder that humans are pretty special.

Where does anxiety end and news begin?

ALL THAT CATASTROPHISING is irrational, but it has an emotional power. And it isn't just folk with anxiety who know this.

Advertisers know it.

Insurance sales people know it.

Politicians know it.

News editors know it.

Political agitators know it.

Terrorists know it.

Sex isn't really what sells. What sells is fear.

And now we don't just have to *imagine* the worst catastrophes. We can see them. Literally. The camera phone has made us all telejournalists. When something truly awful happens – a terrorist incident, a forest fire, a tsunami – people are always there to film it.

We have more food for our nightmares. We don't get our information, as people used to, from one carefully considered newspaper or TV news report. We get it from news sites and social media and email alerts. And besides,

TV news itself isn't what it used to be. Breaking news is continuous. And the more terrifying the news, the higher the ratings.

That doesn't mean all news people *want* bad news. Some do, judging from the divisive way they present it. But even the best news channels want high ratings, and over the years they work out what works and what doesn't, and compete ever harder for attention, which is why watching news can feel like watching a continuous metaphor for generalised anxiety disorder. The various split screens and talking heads and rolling banners of incessant information are a visual representation of how anxiety feels. All that conflicting chatter and noise and sensationalist drama. We can feel stressed watching the news, even on a slow news day. Because, really, there is no longer such a thing as a slow news day.

And when something truly terrible has happened the endless stream of eyewitness accounts and speculation and phone footage does not help anything. It is all sensation and no information. If you find the news severely exacerbates your state of mind, the thing to do is SWITCH IT OFF. Don't let the terror into your mind. No good is done by being paralysed and powerless in front of non-stop rolling news.

The news unconsciously mimics the way fear operates – focusing on the worst things, catastrophising, listening to an endless, repetitive stream of information on the same worrying topic. So, it can be hard to tell these days where your anxiety disorder ends and where actual news begins.

So we have to remember:

There is no shame in *not watching news*.

There is no shame in *not going on Twitter*.

There is no shame in *disconnecting*.

2

THE BIG PICTURE

'We seldom realise, for example, that our most private thoughts and emotions are not actually our own. For we think in terms of languages and images which we did not invent, but which were given to us by our society.'

—Alan Watts, *The Culture of Counter Culture: Edited Transcripts*

Life moves pretty fast

OF COURSE, IN the cosmic perspective, the whole of human history has been *fast*.

We haven't been here long. The planet is around 4.6 billion years old. Our specific and wonderful and problematic species – Homo sapiens – has only been here for 200,000 years. And it was only in the last 50,000 years that things picked up a gear. When we started wearing clothes from animal skins. When we began burying our dead as a matter of practice. When our hunting methods became more advanced.

The oldest known cave art is probably Indonesian and over 40,000 years old. In world terms that was a blink of an eye ago. But art is older than agriculture. Agriculture arrived basically yesterday.

We've only had farms for 10,000 years. And writing has only been around, as far as we know, for a minuscule 5,000 years.

Civilisation, which began in Mesopotamia (roughly Iraq and Syria on today's map), is under 4,000 years old. And once civilisation began, things *really* began to speed up. It was time to fasten our collective seat belts. Money. The first alphabet. The first musical notation system. The pyramids. Buddhism and Hinduism and Christianity and Islam and Sikhism. Socratic philosophy. The concept of democracy. Glass. Swords. Warships. Canals. Roads. Bridges. Schools. Toilet paper. Clocks. Compasses. Bombs. Eyeglasses. Mines. Guns. Better guns. Newspapers. Telescopes. The first piano. Sewing machines. Morphine. Refrigerators. Transatlantic telegraph cables. Rechargeable batteries. Telephones. Cars. Aeroplanes. Ballpoint pens. Jazz. Quiz shows. Coca-Cola. Polyester. Thermonuclear weapons. Rockets to the moon. Personal computers. Video games. Bloody *email*. The world wide web. Nanotechnology.

Whoosh.

But this change – even within the last four millennia – is not a smooth, straight upward line. It is the kind of steepening curve that would intimidate a professional skateboarder. Change may be a constant, but the rate of change is not.

How do you stay human
in a world of change?

WHEN LOOKING AT triggers for mental health problems, therapists often identify an intense change in someone's life as a major factor. Change is frequently related to fear. Moving house, losing a job, getting married, an increase or decrease in income, a death in the family, a diagnosis of a health problem, turning 40, whatever. Sometimes, it doesn't even matter too much if the change is outwardly a 'good' one – having a baby, getting a promotion. The intensity of the change can be a shock to the system.

What, though, when the change isn't just a personal one?

What about when change affects everyone?

What happens when whole societies – or a whole human population – undergo a period of profound change?

What *then*?

These questions are, of course, making an assumption. The assumption is that the world is changing. How is the world changing?

Chiefly, and most measurably, the change is technological.

Yes, there are other social and political and economic and environmental changes, but technology is related to all of them, and underlies them, so let's start with that.

Of course, as a species, we humans have always been shaped by technology. It underpins everything.

Technology, in its baggiest sense, just means tools or methods. It could mean language. It could mean flints or dry sticks used to make fire. According to many anthropologists, technological progress is the most important factor driving human society.

Inventions such as man-made fire, the wheel, the plough or the printing press weren't just important for their immediate purpose but in terms of their overall impact on how societies developed.

In the 19th century, the American anthropologist Lewis H. Morgan announced that technological inventions can lead to whole new eras of humanity. He saw three phases of social evolution – savagery, barbarism and civilisation – with each one leading to the next due to technological leaps forward. This seems a bit dodgy now, I think, because it implies an increasingly questionable moral advancement from 'savages' to the 'civilised'.

Other experts have had different takes.

In the 1960s a Russian alien-hunting astrophysicist named Nikolai Kardashev thought the best way to measure progress was in terms of *information*. In the beginning there was little more than the information contained in our genes. After that came things like language and writing and books and, ultimately, *information technology*.

Nowadays, contemporary sociologists and anthropologists pretty much agree that we are heading deep into a post-industrial society, and that change is happening faster than ever.

But how fast?

According to Moore's Law – named after the co-founder of Intel, Gordon Moore, who forecast it – processing power for computers doubles every few years. This exponential doubling is the reason the small smartphone in your pocket packs way more power than the giant room-sized computers of the 1960s.

But this rapid power growth isn't just confined to computer chips. It occurs across all kinds of technological things, from bits of stored data to internet bandwidth. It all suggests that technology doesn't simply progress – its progress *speeds up*. Progress breeds progress.

Computers now help to build new computers with

increasingly small amounts of human involvement. Which means lots of people have started worrying about – or hoping for – the 'singularity'. This is the stuff of fever dreams and nightmares. The singularity is the point at which artificial intelligence becomes more intelligent than the brainiest human being. And then – depending on your inner optimism-to-pessimism ratio – either we will merge with and advance with this technology, and become immortal and happy cyborgs, *or* our sentient robots and laptops and toasters will take us over and we will be their pets or slaves or three-course meal.

Who knows?

But we are heading in one of those directions. According to world-renowned computer scientist and futurist Ray Kurzweil the singularity is near. To emphasise this point, he even wrote a bestselling book called, well, *The Singularity Is Near*.

At the dawn of this century he claimed that 'we won't experience 100 years of progress in the 21st century – it will be more like 20,000 years of progress (at today's rate)'. And Kurzweil isn't some stoned eccentric, overdosing on sci-fi movies. His predictions have a habit of coming true. For instance, back in 1990 he predicted a computer would beat a chess champion by 1998. People laughed. But then, in

1997, the greatest chess player in the world – Garry Kasparov – lost to IBM's Deep Blue computer.

And just think what has happened in the first two decades of this century. Think how fast normality has shifted.

The internet has taken over our lives. We have become increasingly attached to ever-cleverer smartphones. Human genomes can be sequenced in their thousands by machines.

Self-service checkouts are the new norm. Self-drive cars have gone from far-out prophecy to such an actual real-world business model that taxi drivers fear for their jobs.

Just think. In the year 2000, no one knew what a selfie was. Google did just about exist but it was a long way from becoming a verb. There was no YouTube, no vlogging, no Wikipedia, no WhatsApp, no Snapchat, no Skype, no Spotify, no Siri, no Facebook, no bitcoin, no tweeted gifs, no Netflix, no iPads, no 'lol' or 'ICYMI', no crying-with-laughter emoji, almost no one had sat nav, you generally looked at photographs in *albums*, and the cloud was only ever a thing which produced rain. Even writing this paragraph I sense how quickly it will date. How in a few years there will be so many embarrassing omissions from that list – so many technological brands and inventions which haven't quite arrived. Indeed, think about that. Think how shamefully dated technology becomes in a mere matter of years. Think of fax machines, and old mobile phones, and compact discs, and dial-up modems, and Betamax and VHS, and the first e-readers, and GeoCities and the AltaVista search engine.

So, regardless of what you or I think of the prospect of the singularity, there is no doubt that: a) our lives are becoming ever more technological; and b) our technology is changing at ever increasing speeds.

And, just as technology has always been the deepest root of social change, so this dizzying pace of technological change is triggering other changes. We are heading towards many alternate singularities. Many other points of no return. Maybe we have passed some without even noticing.

Ways the world is changing
that aren't entirely good

THE WORLD MAY have progressed fast in some ways, but the speed of change has not made us all very calm. And some changes, particularly those fuelled by technology, have been faster than others. For instance:

– *Politics*. The polarisation of the political right and left, fuelled in part by our social media echo chambers and gladiatorial combat zones, where compromise and common ground and objective truth seem like ever more outdated concepts. A world where, in the words of American sociologist Sherry Turkle, 'we expect more from technology and less from each other'. Where we need to share ourselves, simply to be ourselves. There have been good aspects to this change. A lot of good causes – including mental health awareness – have had their profile raised thanks to the viral nature of the internet. But, of course, not everything has been so good. The rise of fake news on social media, of politically malicious Twitter bots, and of massive online privacy breaches, has already shaped and steered our politics in strange and irreversible directions.

– *Work*. Robots and computers are taking people's jobs. Employers are taking people's weekends. Employment is becoming a dehumanising process, as if humans existed to serve work, rather than work to serve humans.

– *Social media*. The socialisation of media has rapidly taken over our lives. For those of us using it, our pages on Facebook, Twitter and Instagram are magazines of us. How healthy can that be? We are seeing ever more frequent ethical breaches, such as Cambridge Analytica's illicit harvesting of millions of psychological profiles through Facebook and the company's use of these to influence electoral results. Then there are other serious psychological concerns. To be constantly presenting ourselves, and packaging ourselves, like potatoes pretending to be crisps. To be constantly seeing everyone else looking their best, doing fun things that we are not doing.

– *Language*. The English language is changing faster than at any time in history, according to research carried out by University College London. The growth in text speak and initialisms and acronyms and emojis and gifs as communication aids shows how technological advancements influence language (think also of how, many centuries ago, the printing press led to standardisations of spelling and grammar). So, it's not just what people are saying but how they're saying it. Many millions of people now have more text message conversations than face-to-face ones. This is an unprecedented shift that has taken place within a single generation. It isn't a *bad* thing in itself, but it is definitely a *thing*.

– *Environment*. Some changes, though, are clearly bad. Straightforwardly, horrendously *bad*. The changes to our planet's environment are so grave that some scientists have put forward the idea that we – or our planet – have entered a fundamentally new phase. In 2016, at the International Geological Congress in Cape Town, leading scientists decided that we were leaving the Holocene epoch – one marked by 12,000 years of stable climate since the last Ice Age – and entering something else: the Anthropocene age, or 'new age of man'. The massive acceleration of carbon dioxide emissions, sea-level rises, the pollution of our oceans, the increase in plastic (plastic production has multiplied 20 times since the 1960s, according to the World Economic Forum), the rapid extinction of species, deforestation, industrialised farming and fishing, and urban development mean for those scientists that we have arrived at a new interval of Earth time. So, modern life is, basically, slowly killing the planet. Small wonder that such toxic societies can damage us, too.

Future tense

WHEN PROGRESS HAPPENS fast it can make the present feel like a continual future. When watching a viral clip of a human-sized back-flipping robot, it feels like reality has become science fiction.

And we are encouraged to desire this state of affairs. 'Embrace' the future and 'let go' of the past. The whole of consumerism is based on us wanting the *next thing* rather than the *present thing we already have*. This is an almost perfect recipe for unhappiness.

We are not encouraged to live in the present. We are trained to live somewhere else: the future. We are sent to kindergarten or *pre*-school, which by its very nature reminds us of what is about to hit us. *School* school. And once there, from an increasingly early age, we are encouraged to work hard so we pass tests. Eventually, these tests evolve into actual exams, which we know will dictate important future things like whether we pursue further education or decide to get a job at the age of sixteen or eighteen. Even if we go to university, it doesn't stop there. There will be more tests, more exams, more looming decisions. More *where do you see yourself in a few years' time?* More *what career path would you like to pursue?* More *think very carefully about your future.* More *it will all pay off in the long run.*

All through our education we are being taught a kind of reverse mindfulness. A kind of Future Studies where – via the guise of mathematics, or literature, or history, or computer programming, or French – we are being taught to think of a time different to the time we are in. Exam time. Job time. When-we-are-grown-up time.

To see the act of learning as something not for its own sake but because of what it will *get* you reduces the wonder of humanity. We are thinking, feeling, art-making, knowledge-hungry, marvellous animals, who understand ourselves and our world through the act of learning. It is an end in itself. It has far more to offer than the things it lets us write on application forms. It is a way to love living right now.

I am coming to realise how wrong many of my aspirations have been. How locked out of the present I have found myself. How I have always wanted *more* of whatever was in front of me. I need to find a way to stay still, in the present, and, as my nan used to say, *be happy with what you have.*

Goalposts

YOU WILL BE happy when you get good grades.

You will be happy when you go to university. You will be happy when you go to the *right* university. You will be happy when you get a job. You will be happy when you get a pay rise. You will be happy when you get a promotion. You will be happy when you can work for yourself. You will be happy when you are rich. You will be happy when you own an olive grove in Sardinia.

You will be happy when someone looks at you *that way*. You will be happy when you are in a relationship. You will be happy when you get married. You will be happy when you have children. You will be happy when your children are exactly the kind of children you want them to be.

You will be happy when you leave home. You will be happy when you buy a house. You will be happy when you pay off the mortgage. You will be happy when you have a bigger garden. In the countryside. With nice neighbours who invite you to barbecues on sunny Saturdays in July, with your children playing together in the warm breeze.

You will be happy to sing. You will be happy to sing in front of a crowd. You will be happy when your Grammy-winning debut album is number one in 32 countries, including Latvia.

You will be happy to write. You will happy to be published. You will be happy to be published *again*. You will happy to have a bestseller. You will be happy to have a number *one* bestseller. You will be happy when they turn your book into a movie. You will be happy when they turn it into a *great* movie. You will be happy when you are J.K. Rowling.

You will be happy when people like you. You will be happy when *more* people like you. You will be happy when *everyone* likes you. You will be happy when people *dream* of you.

You will be happy to look okay. You will be happy to turn heads. You will be happy with smoother skin. You will be happy with a flat stomach. You will be happy with a six-pack. You will be happy with an eight-pack. You will be happy when every photo of yourself gets 10,000 likes on Instagram.

You will be happy when you have transcended earthly woes. You will be happy when you are at one with the universe. You will be happy when you are the universe.

You will be happy when you are a god. You will be happy when you are the god to rule all gods. You will be happy when you are Zeus. In the clouds above Mount Olympus, commanding the sky.

Maybe. Maybe.

Maybe.

Maybe

MAYBE HAPPINESS IS not about us, as individuals. Maybe it is not something that arrives *into* us. Maybe happiness is felt heading out, not in. Maybe happiness is not about what we deserve *because we're worth it*. Maybe happiness is not about what we can *get*. Maybe happiness is about what we already *have*. Maybe happiness is about what we can *give*. Maybe happiness is not a butterfly we can catch with a net. Maybe there is no certain way to be happy. Maybe there are only maybes. If (as Emily Dickinson said) 'Forever – is composed of Nows –', maybe the nows are made of maybes. Maybe the point of life is to give up certainty and to embrace life's beautiful uncertainty.

3

A FEELING IS
NOT YOUR FACE

'It's such a weird thing for young people to look at distorted images of things they should be.'

—Daisy Ridley, on why she quit Instagram

Unhappy beauties

NEVER IN HUMAN history have so many products and services been available to make ourselves achieve the goal of looking more young and attractive.

Day creams, night creams, neck creams, hand creams, exfoliators, spray tans, mascaras, anti-age serums, cellulite creams, face masks, concealers, shaving creams, beard trimmers, foundations, lipsticks, home waxing kits, recovery oils, pore correctors, eyeliners, Botox, manicures, pedicures, microdermabrasion (a strange cross between modern exfoliation and medieval torture, by the sound of it), mud baths, seaweed wraps and full-blown plastic surgery. There are facial-hair trimmers and nose-hair trimmers and pubic-hair trimmers (or 'body groomers'). You can even bleach your anus if the mood so takes you. ('Intimate bleaching' is a thriving sub-market.)

In this age of the beauty blog and make-up vlogger and online workout instructor, there has never been such a plethora of advice on looking good. We are bombarded with diet books, and gym memberships, and 'dream abs' workouts and 'action hero' workouts and 'face yoga' videos we can access via YouTube. And there are ever more digital apps and filters to enhance what the products can't. If we so desire we can make ourselves into our own unrealistic aspirations and create an ever wider gap between what we can see in a mirror and what we can digitally enhance. Women – and increasingly men – are doing more than ever to improve their appearance.

Yet, despite all our new methods and tricks to look better, a lot of us remain unhappy with our looks. The largest global study of its kind, conducted by research group GfK and published in *Time* magazine back in 2015, suggested that millions of people were not satisfied with how they look. In Japan, for instance, 38 per cent of people were found to be seriously unhappy about their appearance. The interesting thing about the survey was that it showed that how you feel about your looks is surprisingly far more determined by the nation in which you live than by, say, your gender. In fact, all over the world, levels of anxiety about how you look are moving towards being as high in men as they are in women.

If you are Mexican or Turkish, you are likely to be fine about what you see in the mirror, as over 70 per cent of people there are 'completely satisfied' or 'fairly satisfied' with their looks. People in Japan, Britain, Russia and South Korea were much more likely to be miserable.

So why are so many people – with the exception of Mexicans and Turkish people – unhappy with their looks? A few reasons, it seems:

1. While we have an increased ability to look better than ever before, we also have much higher standards of what we want to look like.

2. We are bombarded with more images of conventionally beautiful people than ever before. Not just via TV and cinema screens and billboards, but via social media, where everyone presents their best, most filtered selves to show the world.

3. As people become more neurotic generally, worries about appearance increase. According to the authors of another survey (for the American National Center for Biotechnology Information in 2017), people who were unhappy with their looks had 'higher neuroticism, more preoccupied and fearful attachment styles and spent more hours watching television'.

4. Our looks are presented as one of the problems that can be fixed by spending money (on cosmetics, fitness magazines, the right food, gym membership, whatever).

But this is not true. And besides, looking convention-ally attractive does not make you stop worrying about your looks. There are as many good-looking people in Japan and Russia as Mexico and Turkey. And, of course, many very good-looking people – models, for instance – are more worried about their looks than people who don't walk down catwalks for a living.

5. We still aren't immortal. All these products aiming to make us look younger and glowing and less death-like are not addressing the root problem. They can't actually make us younger. Clarins and Clinique have produced a ton of anti-ageing creams and yet the people who use them are still going to age. They are just – thanks in part to the billion-dollar marketing campaigns aimed at making us ashamed of wrinkles and lines and ageing – a bit more worried about it. The pursuit of looking young accentuates the fear of growing old. So maybe if we embraced growing old, embraced our wrinkles and other people's wrinkles, maybe marketers would have less fear to work with and magnify.

Insecurity is not about your face

I USED TO be the tallest boy in my school and skinny as a rake. I binge-ate and drank beer just to get bigger. I probably had a bit of body dysmorphia, I now realise. I was unhappy in my own skin. And *with* my own skin. I used to do sets of 50 press-ups, wincing through the pain, trying to look like Jean-Claude Van Damme. Not just disliking my body, actively *hating* it. A real intense physical shame that sometimes people imagine only girls and women can feel. I wish I could go back through time and tell myself, *Stop this. None of this matters. Chill out.*

I once hated a mole on my face so much that, as a teenager, I took a toothbrush to it and tried to scrub it off. But the problem was never the mole. The problem was that I was viewing my own face through the prism of my insecurity. I like that mole now. I have no idea why it used to trouble me so much, why I would stare at it in the mirror, wishing it into non-existence.

As Hamlet said to Rosencrantz, 'there is nothing either good or bad, but thinking makes it so'. He was talking about Denmark. But it applies to our looks, too. People might be encouraged to feel inadequate, but they don't have to, as soon as they realise that the *feeling* is separate from the *thing* they are worried about. So, while there is a lot of awareness about the dangers of obesity, there seems to be less awareness of the other kind of problems with our physical appearance. If we are feeling bad about our looks, sometimes the thing we need to address is the feeling, not our actual physical appearance.

Professor Pamela Keel of Florida State University has spent her career studying eating disorders and issues around female and male body image, and concludes that changing the way you look is never going to solve unhappiness about your looks. 'What is really going to make you happier and healthier?' she wondered at the start of 2018, presenting her latest research findings. 'Losing ten pounds or losing harmful attitudes about your body?' And when people feel less pressure about how their bodies look, it's not just minds that benefit, but bodies too. 'When people feel good about their bodies, they are more likely to take better care of themselves rather than treating their bodies like an enemy, or even worse, an object. That's a powerful reason to rethink the kind of New Year's resolutions we make.'

This might explain why rates of obesity are themselves dangerously rising. If we were happier with our bodies, we'd be kinder to them.

Just as being overly anxious about money can paradoxically result in compulsive spending, so worrying about our bodies is no guarantee we'll have better bodies.

The pressure on people to worry about how they look, to eat 'clean', to consider things like thigh gaps, to have 'beach ready' bodies, has been traditionally very gender-focused, with advertisers putting much more pressure on women. And even now, as increasing numbers of men feel the pressure to look a way that is not how most men naturally look, to have gym-defined bodies, to be ashamed of their physical flaws, to look good in selfies, to worry about their hair going grey or falling out, the pressure on women to fret about their appearance has never been greater. Instead of trying to reduce women's appearance-related anxiety, we are raising men's appearance-related anxiety. In some areas, in some kind of distorted idea of equality, we seem to be trying to make everyone equally anxious, rather than equally free.

Just a moment ago, as I looked at Twitter, I saw someone retweet an article from the *New York Post* captioned 'Male sex dolls with bionic penises will be here before

2019'. There is a picture of these sex dolls – hairless and impossibly toned bodies, complete with hair that will never fall out and penises that will never fail to be erect. Of course, inevitably, bionic female sex robots are being advanced, too, with even greater zeal. Now, wanting to look like a photoshopped model on the cover of a magazine is one thing. But will the next stage be wanting to look as blandly perfect as an android or robot? We might as well try to catch rainbows.

'In nature,' wrote Alice Walker, 'nothing is perfect and everything is perfect. Trees can be contorted, bent in weird ways, and they're still beautiful.' Our bodies will never be as firm and symmetrical and ageless as those of bionic sex robots, so we need quite quickly to learn how to be happy with not having society's unrealistic version of the 'best' body, and a bit happier with having *our* body, as it is, not least because being unhappy with our body doesn't make us look any better. It just makes us feel a lot worse. We are infinitely better than the most perfect-looking bionic sex robots. We are humans. Let's not be ashamed to look like them.

A note from the beach

Hello.

I am the beach.

I am created by waves and currents.

I am made of eroded rocks.

I exist next to the sea.

I have been around for millions of years.

I was around at the dawn of life itself.

And I have to tell you something.

I don't care about your body.

I am a beach.

I literally don't give a fuck.

I am entirely indifferent to your body mass
   index.

I am not impressed that your abdominal
   muscles are visible to the naked eye.

I am oblivious.

You are one of 200,000 generations of human beings.

I have seen them all.

I will see all the generations that come after you, too.

It won't be as many. I'm sorry.

I hear the whispers the sea tells me.

(The sea hates you. The *poisoners*. That's what it calls you. A bit melodramatic, I know. But that's the sea for you. All drama.)

And I have to tell you something else.

Even the other people on the beach don't care about your body.

They don't.

They are staring at the sea, or they are obsessed with *their own* appearance.

And if they *are* thinking about you, why do you care? Why do you humans worry so much about a stranger's opinion?

Why don't you do what I do? Let it wash all over you. Allow yourself just to be *as you are*.

Just be.

Just beach.

How to stop worrying about ageing

1. Understand that old people aren't actually that worried about old age, according to numerous surveys. The most recent one I can find was undertaken by American research firm NORC in 2016. It polled over 3,000 adults and found that old people are more optimistic about growing old than younger adults: 46 per cent of thirty-somethings said they were optimistic about ageing, compared to 66 per cent for the seventy pluses. It seems that worrying about growing old is a sign you are young. And the main reason to be optimistic about old age is that old people themselves are. Resilience seems to grow.

2. It happens. Ageing is something we can't do much about. We can eat healthily, exercise and live sensibly but we will still *age*. Our 80th birthday will still be on the same date. Sure, we can make it more likely we will reach 80, but we can't stop the wheels of time. And the certainty is actually quite reassuring. When there is nothing we can do about something, the point of worry begins to diminish. 'Everybody dies,' wrote Nora

Ephron. 'There's nothing you can do about it. Whether or not you eat six almonds a day.'

3. The problems you associate with old age might not be the problems you have. You aren't Nostradamus. You don't know what you will be like when you are old. You don't know, for instance, if your mind will decline or if it will shine ever brighter, like Matisse, who produced some of his best works of art in his eighties.

4. The future isn't real. The future is abstract. The now is all we know. One now after another now. The now is where we must live. There are billions of different versions of an older you. There is one version of the present you. Focus on that.

5. You will regret the fear. In *The Top Five Regrets of the Dying,* Bronnie Ware – a nurse who worked in palliative care – shared her experience of talking to those near the end of their lives. Far and away the biggest regret they had was *fear.* Many of Bronnie's patients were in deep anguish that they had spent their whole lives worrying. Lives consumed by fear. Worrying what other people thought of them. A worry that had stopped them being true to themselves.

6. Embrace, don't resist. The way to get rid of age anxiety might be the way you get rid of all anxiety. By

acceptance, not *denial*. Don't fight it, feel it. Maybe don't inject yourself with Botox. Do some knifeless mental surgery instead. Reframe your idea of beauty. Be a rebel against marketing. Look forward to being the wise elder. Be the complex elegance of a melting candle. Be a map with 10,000 roads. Be the orange at sunset that outclasses the pink of sunrise. Be the self that dares to be true.

4
NOTES ON TIME

Fear and time

'THE ONLY THING we have to fear is fear itself.' That phrase, first uttered by Franklin D. Roosevelt in 1932 during his inaugural speech as president, is probably the one I have thought about most in my life. It used to taunt me, during my first bout of panic disorder. Fear is enough, I used to think. The words have also been in my mind while writing this book. Like 'time heals' and all the best clichés, it has become a cliché for good reason – it has the power of truth.

When I think about my own fears, most of them are to do with time itself. I worry about ageing. I worry about our children ageing. I worry about the future. I worry about losing people. I worry I am late with my work. Even writing this book I worry I will fall behind deadline. I worry about the time I have spent unwisely. The time I have spent ill. And, while researching, I began to wonder about whether our concept of time is itself temporal. Has our attitude to time changed? Is the way to be free from fear to come to a new relationship with the tick-tock of minutes and hours and years? I feel if I can begin to understand the way my mind – and maybe your mind – reacts to the modern world, I need to look at time itself.

Stop the clocks

WE DIDN'T ALWAYS have clocks. For most of human history the concept of, say, 'a quarter to five' or 'four forty-five' would have been meaningless.

No one has ever found a Neolithic cave painting of someone waking up stressed because they slept through their alarm and missed their nine o'clock management meeting. Once upon a time, there were really just two times. Day and night. Light and dark. Awake and asleep. Of course, there were other times, too. There were meal times and hunting times and times to fight and times to relax and times to play and times to kiss, but these times weren't dictated artificially by clocks and their numbers and endless partitions.

When time-keeping methods were first used they typically still kept this dual structure sacred. After all, when the Ancient Egyptians looked at the shadows from their time-telling obelisks, or when the Romans looked at their sundials, they could only do so in daylight. Even when mechanical clocks first appeared in Europe in the early

14th century, on things like churches, they were quite casual affairs. They generally didn't have minute hands, for instance, and couldn't be seen from most bedroom windows.

Pocket watches first came about during the 16th century and, like so many consumer desirables, were exclusive status symbols to begin with – novelties for the nobility. A fancy pocket watch in the middle of that century cost in the region of £15, which was more than a farm labourer earned in a year. All that for a watch that didn't even have a minute hand. It was, however, the pocket watch that seemed to make people become a bit antsier about time. Or, at least, antsier about *checking* the time.

When the diarist Samuel Pepys first treated himself to a pocket watch – 'a very fine [one] it is' – in London in 1665 he quickly realised – like so many modern internet users – that having access to information gives you one kind of freedom at the expense of another. He wrote in his diary on 13 May:

But, Lord! to see how much of my old folly and childishnesse hangs upon me still that I cannot forbear carrying my watch in my hand in the coach all this afternoon, and seeing what o'clock it is one hundred times; and am apt to think with myself, how could I be so long without one; though I remember since, I had one, and found it a trouble, and resolved to carry one no more about me while I lived.

Surely anyone who has ever had a smartphone or a Twitter account can relate to such compulsive behaviour. Check, check, check, and once more, just to see. When the ability to check something turns into the compulsion to do so, we often find ourselves craving the time before, when there was no ability to check in the first place.

The thing is, Pepys' pocket watch wasn't even very good. It wasn't even *quite* good. It was a very crap piece of tech for a year's salary. But no pocket watch in 1665 was good, at least not at telling the time. It wasn't until a decade later with the invention of the hairspring, which controlled the speed of the watch's balance wheel, that even vaguely accurate pocket watches were possible.

Since then, of course, our ways of measuring time have become ever more advanced. We are now in the age of atomic clocks. These are incredibly, intimidatingly accurate clocks. For instance, in 2016, physicists in Germany built a clock so accurate that it won't lose or gain a second for 15 billion years. German physicists now have no excuse for being late for anything ever again.

We are too aware of numerical time and not aware enough of natural time. People for thousands of years may have woken up at seven in the morning. The difference with these last few centuries is that now we are waking up *because* it is seven in the morning. We go to school or college or work at a certain time of day, not because that feels the most natural time to do so, but because that is the time that has been given to us. We have handed over our instincts to the hands of a clock. Increasingly, we serve time rather than time serving us. We fret about time. We wonder where time has gone. We are obsessed with time.

A phone call

'MATTHEW?' IT'S MY mum. She is the only one who ever calls me Matthew.

'Yeah.'

'Were you listening to what I was saying?'

'Um. Yeah. Something about going to the doctor . . .'

Shamefully, I hadn't been listening. I was staring at an email I was halfway through writing. So, I change strategy. I tell her the truth.

'I'm sorry. I'm just on the laptop. I'm very busy. I seem to have no time at all at the moment . . .'

Mum sighs, and I hear the sigh instantaneously, even though she is 200 miles away. 'I know the feeling.'

We need the time we already have

THE THING IS, we should have more time than ever. I mean, think about it. Life expectancy has more than doubled for people living in the developed world during the last century. And not only that, we have more time-saving devices and technologies than ever before existed.

Emails are faster than letters. Electric heaters are faster than fires. Washing machines are speedier than hand-washing over a sink or a river. Once laborious processes like waiting for your hair to dry or travelling ten miles or boiling water or searching through data now take next to no time at all. We have time- and effort-saving things like tractors and cars and washing machines and production lines and microwave ovens.

And yet, for a lot of our lives we feel rushed off our feet. We say things like 'I'd love to read more/learn a musical instrument/go to the gym/do some charity work/cook my own meals/grow strawberries/see my old school friends/train for a marathon . . . *if only I had the time.*'

We often find ourselves wishing for more hours in the day, but that wouldn't help anything. The problem, clearly, isn't that we have a shortage of time. It's more that we have an overload of *everything else*.

Remember

Feeling you have no time doesn't mean you have no time.

Feeling you are ugly doesn't mean you are ugly.

Feeling anxious doesn't mean you need to be anxious.

Feeling you haven't achieved enough doesn't mean you haven't achieved enough.

Feeling you lack things doesn't make you less complete.

5
LIFE OVERLOAD

An excess of everything

THERE IS, IN the current world, an excess of *everything*.

Think of just one single category of thing.

Think, say, of the thing you are holding – a book.

There are *a lot* of books. You have, for whatever reason, chosen to read this one, for which I sincerely thank you. But while you are reading this book you might also be painfully aware that you aren't reading other books. And I don't want to stress you out too much but there are *a lot* of other books. The website Mental Floss, relying heavily on data from Google, calculated there were – at a conservative estimate – 134,021,533 books in existence, but that was halfway through 2016. There are many millions more now. And anyway, 134,021,533 is still, technically, *a lot*.

It wasn't always like this.

We didn't always have so many books, and there was an obvious reason. Before printing presses books had to be made by hand, written on surfaces of clay, papyrus, wax or parchment.

Even after the printing press was invented there wasn't that much stuff to read. A book club in England in the early 16th century would have struggled as there were only around 40 different books published a year, according to figures from the British Library. An avid reader could therefore quite easily keep up with every book that was published.

'So, what are ye all reading?' a hypothetical member of the hypothetical book club would ask.

'Whatever there is, Cedric,' would be the reply.

However, the situation changed quite quickly. By the year 1600 there were around 400 different titles being published per year in England – a tenfold increase on the previous century.

Although it is said that the poet Samuel Taylor Coleridge was the last person who read everything, this is a technical impossibility as he died in 1834, when there were already millions of books in existence. However, what is interesting is that people of the time could *believe* it was possible to read everything. No one could believe such a thing now.

We all know that, even if we break the world record for speed reading, the number of books we read will only ever be a minuscule fraction of the books in existence. We are drowning in books just as we are drowning in TV shows. And yet we can only read one book – and watch one TV show – at a time. We have multiplied everything, but we are still individual selves. There is only one of us. And we are all smaller than an internet. To enjoy life, we might have to stop thinking about what we will never be able to read and watch and say and do, and start to think of how to enjoy the world within our boundaries. To live on a human scale. To focus on the few things we can do, rather than the millions of things we can't. To not crave parallel lives. To find a smaller mathematics. To be a proud and singular one. An indivisible prime.

The world is having a panic attack

PANIC IS A kind of overload.

That is how my panic attacks used to feel. An excess of thought and fear. An overloaded mind reaches a breaking point and the panic floods in. Because that overload makes you feel trapped. Psychologically boxed in. That is why panic attacks often happen in over-stimulating environments. Supermarkets and nightclubs and theatres and overcrowded trains.

But what happens when overload becomes a central characteristic of modern life? Consumer overload. Work overload. Environmental overload. News overload. Information overload.

The challenge today, then, is not that life is necessarily worse than it once was. In many ways, human lives have the potential to be better and healthier and even happier than in eras past. The trouble is our lives are also cluttered. The challenge is to find who we are amid the crowd of ourselves.

Places I have had
panic attacks

Supermarkets.

The windowless basement floor of a department store.

A packed music festival.

At a nightclub.

On an aeroplane.

On the London underground.

In a tapas bar in Seville.

In the *BBC News* green room.

On a train from London to York (it lasted most of the journey).

In a cinema.

In a theatre.

At a corner shop.

On a stage, feeling unnatural, with a thousand faces staring at me.

Walking through Covent Garden.

Watching the TV.

At home, very late at night, after a busy day, with a

streetlight glowing an ominous orange through the curtains.

In a bank.

In front of a computer screen.

A nervous planet

'IMAGINE IF THE world didn't simply make people mad,' a friend said to me recently, after I'd told him about the book I was trying to write. 'Imagine if the world was itself mad. Or, you know, the bits of the world to do with us. Humans. I mean, what if it is *literally mad*. I think that's what is happening. I think human society is breaking down.'

'Yes. Like a patient having a nervous breakdown.'

'Yeah. I mean, obviously the world isn't a person. But it is increasingly connected, like you say – like a nervous system. Been like that a while, in fact. There was a guy I was reading about, in the 19th century. He said that all the telegraph cables were like a nervous system.'

On further research, I found the man was called Charles Tilston Bright – the man in charge of the first transatlantic telegraph cable. He referred to the global telegraph network as 'the world's system of electrical nerves'.

We no longer have telegraphs as such, as they didn't prove too good at posting ninja cat videos and emojis.

But the world's nervous system has not gone away. It has evolved in scale and complexity to the extent that, since June 2017, over half the world's population is connected to the internet, according to figures from the United Nations International Telecommunications Union (which, incidentally, used to be the International *Telegraph* Union).

The number of internet users has been growing rapidly, year by year. It's wild to think that back in 1995 comparatively no one was on the internet: 16 million people, just 0.4 per cent of the world population. A decade later, in 2005, it was up to a billion people, which meant 15 per cent of the world's population was online. And by 2017 those digits flipped to 51 per cent.

In that same year the number of active Facebook users – people who use Facebook at least once a month – reached *2.07 billion*. At the start of this decade, back in 2010, there weren't even that many people on the entire internet. This is a *rapid* amount of change. It has happened because many parts of the world have 'modernised' and have changed their infrastructure quickly to make way for broadband internet. The other factor is the rise of the smartphone, which has made accessing the internet far easier than it used to be.

And it's not just the amount of people who use the internet that is rising, the amount of time we spend online is rising too.

Human beings are more connected via technology than ever before, and this radical change has happened in little over a decade. And, if nothing else, it's leading to a lot of arguments online. As Tolstoy wrote, back in 1894, in *The Kingdom of God Is Within You*:

> The more men are freed from privation; the more telegraphs, telephones, books, papers, and journals there are; the more means there will be of diffusing inconsistent lies and hypocrisies, and the more disunited and consequently miserable will men become, which indeed is what we see actually taking place.

And things are happening too quickly for us to take stock of it all. Certainly quicker than in Tolstoy's time. All this falling out. All this information. All this technological connection. The world's brain is a common but fitting metaphor. We are the nerve cells of the world's brain, transmitting ourselves to all the other nerve cells. Sending the overload back and forth. Overloaded neurons on a nervous planet. Ready to crash.

6

INTERNET ANXIETIES

'The Internet is the first thing that humanity has built that humanity doesn't understand, the largest experiment in anarchy that we have ever had.'

—Eric Schmidt, former CEO of Google

'A handful of people, working at a handful of technology companies, through their choices will steer what a billion people are thinking today . . . I don't know a more urgent problem than this . . . It's changing our democracy, and it's changing our ability to have the conversations and relationships that we want with each other.'

—Tristan Harris, former Google employee

Things I love about
the internet

Collective action against social injustice.

Watching old pop videos I had forgotten about.

Watching movie trailers without having to be in a cinema.

Wikipedia, Spotify, BBC Good Food recipes.

The process of researching a trip away.

Goodreads.

Finding people who understand what you feel like when you are low.

Talking to readers I would otherwise never talk to.

Friendliness, which does happen quite a lot.

Watching videos of animals doing incredible things (a gorilla dancing in a pool, an octopus opening a jar).

Being able to go up to people via email or a message in a way I wouldn't be able to in real life.

Funny tweets.

Staying in touch with old friends.

The ability to test out ideas with people.

Really good yoga instructors from Austin, Texas, whose practices I can follow without living in Austin, Texas.

Equally good cool-down stretch running videos.

Researching the downsides of the internet, via the internet.

Things I should do less of on the internet

Post about a meaningful experience, when I could be having an actual meaningful experience.

Write tweets containing opinions that will win nobody over.

Click on articles I don't really want to read.

Browse my Twitter feed when I should be eating breakfast.

Read my Amazon reviews.

Compare my life to the lives of other people.

Stare at emails without answering them.

Answer emails while I should be listening to my mum talk about her trip to see a doctor.

Feel the empty joy of likes and favourites.

Search my own name.

Click off videos for songs I like on YouTube without waiting until the end, because I have seen another video I like.

Google symptoms and self-diagnose (just because you are a hypochondriac it doesn't mean you aren't actually dying).

Google things – *any* things ('number of atoms in a human body', 'turmeric health benefits', 'cast of *West Side Story*', 'how to download photos from iCloud') – after midnight.

Check how a tweet/photo/status update is going down (and keep checking).

Want to go offline, without going offline.

The world is shrinking

LIFE OVERLOAD IS a feeling that partly stems from how contracted and concentrated the world seems to have become. The human world has sped up and has effectively shrunk, too. It is becoming more connected, and as it becomes more connected, so are we. The 'hive mind' – first coined in a science fiction short story, 'Second Night of Summer' by James H. Schmitz, in 1950 – is now a reality. Our lives, information and emotions are connected in ways they have never been before. The internet is unifying even as it seems to divide.

This shrinking of the world hasn't been an overnight process. Humans have been communicating further than their voices allow for centuries. Using everything from smoke signals to drums to pigeons. A chain of signal beacons from Plymouth to London announced the arrival of the Spanish Armada.

In the 19th century the electrical telegraph connected continents.

Then the global nervous system evolved with the telephone, radio, television and, of course, the internet.

These connections are, in many ways, making us ever closer. We can email or text or Skype or Facetime or play multiplayer online games in real time with people 10,000 miles away. Physical distance is increasingly irrelevant. Social media has enabled collective action like never before, from riots to revolutions to shock election results. The internet has enabled us to join together and make change happen. For better and for worse.

The trouble is that if we are plugged in to a vast nervous system, our happiness – and misery – is more collective than ever. The group's emotions become our own.

Mass hysterics

THERE ARE THOUSANDS of examples in history of individuals getting their emotions influenced by the crowd, from the Salem witch trials to Beatlemania.

One of the most amusing/frightening examples is the case of the French convent in the 15th century where a nun began to miaow like a cat. Pretty soon, other nuns started to miaow, too. And within a few months the nearby villagers were startled to hear *all* the nuns miaowing for several hours a day in a loud cat chorus. They only stopped miaowing when the local authorities threatened to whip them.

There are other odd examples. Such as the Dancing Plague of 1518, where, over the course of a month, 400 people in Strasbourg danced themselves to the point of collapse – and in some cases death – for no understandable reason. No music was even playing.

Or during the Napoleonic Wars when, legend has it, the inhabitants of Hartlepool, England, collectively convinced themselves that a shipwrecked monkey was a French spy and hanged the poor, confused primate. Fake news has been around for a while.

And now, of course, we have a technology – the internet – that makes collective group behaviour more possible and more likely. Different things – songs, tweets, cat videos – go viral on a daily, or hourly, basis. The word 'viral' is perfect at describing the contagious effect caused by the combination of human nature and technology. And, of course, it isn't just videos and products and tweets that can be contagious. Emotions can be, too.

A completely connected world has the potential to go mad, all at once.

Baby steps

IT WAS THE same again. 'Matt, get off the internet.'

Andrea was right, and she was only looking after me, but I didn't want to hear it.

'It's fine.'

'It's not fine. You're having an argument with someone. You're writing a book about how to cope with the stress of the internet and you're getting stressed on the internet.'

'That's not really what it's about. I'm trying to understand how our minds are affected by modernity. I'm writing about the world *as a nervous planet*. How our psychology is connected. I'm writing about all aspects of a—'

She held up her palm. 'Okay. I don't want the TED talk.'

I sighed. 'I'm just getting back to an email.'

'No. No, you aren't.'

'Okay. I'm on Twitter. But there's one point I've just got to get across—'

'Matt, it's up to you. But I thought the whole idea was that you were doing all this to try to work out how not to get like this.'

'Like what?'

'So wrapped up in stuff you shouldn't be wrapped up in. I just don't want you ill. This is how you get ill. That's all.'

She left the room. I stared at the tweet I was about to post. It wasn't going to add anything to my life. Or anyone else's life. It was just going to lead to more checking of my phone, like Pepys with his pocket watch. I pressed delete, and felt a strange relief as I watched each letter disappear.

An ode to social media

When anger trawls the internet,
Looking for a hook;
It's time to disconnect,
And go and read a book.

Mirrors

NEUROBIOLOGISTS HAVE IDENTIFIED 'mirroring' as one of the neural routes activated in the brains of primates – including us – during interaction with others.

In a connected age, the mirrors get bigger.

When people feel scared after a horrific event, that fear spreads like a digital wildfire.

When people feel angry, that anger breeds.

Even when people with contradictory opinions to us exhibit an emotion, we can feel a similar one. For instance, if someone is furious at you online for something, you are unlikely to adopt their opinion but it is quite likely you will catch their fury. You see it every day on social media: people arguing with each other, entrenching each other's opposing view, yet also mirroring each other's emotional state.

I have done this many times, which is why Andrea was frustrated with me. I have become embroiled in some argument with someone who has called me a 'snowflake' or 'libtard' or who has tweet-shouted 'LIBERALISM IS A MENTAL DISORDER' at me. I kind of know that arguing with people online is not the most fulfilling way to spend our limited days on this earth and yet I have done it, without much control. I recognise this now. And I need to stop it.

Anyway, my point is that while I am politically very different to the people I argue with, psychologically we are fuelling each other with the same feelings of anger. Political opposition but emotional mirroring.

I once tweeted something silly in a state of anxiety.

'Anxiety is my superpower,' I said.

I didn't mean anxiety was a *good thing*. I meant that anxiety was ridiculously intense, that we people who have an excess of it walk through life like an anxious Clark Kent or a tormented Bruce Wayne knowing the secret of who we are. And that it can be a burden of racing uncontrollable thoughts and despair but one, just occasionally, that we can convince ourselves has a silver lining.

For instance, personally I am thankful that it forced me to stop smoking, to get physically healthy, that it made me work out what was good for me, and who cared for me and who didn't. I am thankful that it led me to trying to help some other people who experience it, and I am thankful that it led me – during good patches – to feel life more intensely.

It was essentially what I had written in *Reasons to Stay Alive*. But I hadn't expressed it very well in this tweet. And then, suddenly, I was getting a lot of attention on Twitter.

I decided to delete my tweet, but people had screen-grabbed it and were rallying the ranks of the Twitter angry to direct their ire in my direction. 'SUPERPOWER???? WTF!!!' '@matthaig1 IS TOXIC' 'Delete your account' 'What a fucking idiot' and so on. And you stay on, scared, watching this car crash of your own making, as your timeline fills with tens then hundreds of angry people, convinced that as they were touching a raw nerve they had a point. By the way, 'touched a raw nerve' is an irrelevant phrase if you have anxiety. Every nerve feels raw.

The anger became contagious and I could feel it almost like a physical force radiating from the screen. My heart started to beat twice as fast. Everything felt like it was closing in. The air got thinner. I was backed into a corner. I began to feel a bit like reality was melting away. 'Oh shit, oh shit, oh shit.' I lost myself in a brief panic attack. I felt an unhealthy fusion of guilt and fear and defensive anger, and became determined never to live-tweet my way out of anxiety again.

Some things are best kept to yourself.

But also – more importantly – I wanted to find a way to stop other people's view of me becoming *my* view of me. I wanted to create some emotional immunity. Social media, when you get too wrapped up in it, can make you feel like you are inside a stock exchange where you – or your online personality – is the stock. And when people start piling on, you feel your personal share price plummet. I wanted free of that. I wanted to psychologically disconnect myself. To be a self-sustaining market, psychologically speaking. To be comfortable with my own mistakes, knowing that every human is more than them. To allow myself to realise I know my inner workings better than a stranger does. To be able for other people to think I was a wanker, without me feeling I was one. To care about other people, but not about their misreadings of me within the opinion matrix of the internet.

How to stay sane on the internet: a list of utopian commandments I rarely follow, because they are so damn difficult

1. Practise abstinence. Social media abstinence, especially. Resist whatever unhealthy excesses you feel drawn towards. Strengthen those muscles of restraint.

2. Don't type symptoms into Google unless you want to spend seven hours convinced you will be dead before dinner.

3. Remember no one really cares what you look like. They care what *they* look like. You are the only person in the world to have worried about your face.

4. Understand that what seems real might not be. When the novelist William Gibson first imagined the idea of what he coined 'cyberspace' in 1982's 'Burning Chrome', he pictured it as a 'consensual hallucination'. I find this description useful when I am getting too caught up in technology. When it is affecting my non-digital life. The whole internet is one step removed from the physical world. The most powerful

aspects of the internet are mirrors of the offline world, but replications of the external world aren't the actual external world. It is the real internet, but that's all it can be. Yes, you can make real friends on there. But non-digital reality is still a useful test for that friendship. As soon as you step away from the internet – for a minute, an hour, a day, a week – it is surprising how quickly it disappears from your mind.

5. Understand people are more than a social media post. Think how many conflicting thoughts you have in a day. Think of the different contradictory positions you have held in your life. Respond to online opinions but never let one rushed opinion define a whole human being. 'Every one of us,' said the physicist Carl Sagan, 'is, in the cosmic perspective, precious. If a human disagrees with you, let him live. In a hundred billion galaxies, you will not find another.'

6. Don't hate-follow people. This has been my promise to myself since New Year's Day, 2018, and so far it is working. Hate-following doesn't give your righteous anger a focus. It fuels it. In a weird way, it also reinforces your echo chamber by making you feel like the only other opinions are extreme ones. Do not seek out stuff that makes you unhappy. Do not measure your own worth

against other people. Do not seek to define yourself *against*. Define what you are *for*. And browse accordingly.

7. Don't play the ratings game. The internet loves ratings, whether it is reviews on Amazon and TripAdvisor and Rotten Tomatoes, or the ratings of photos and updates and tweets. Likes, favourites, retweets. Ignore it. Ratings are no sign of worth. Never judge yourself on them. To be liked by everyone you would have to be the blandest person ever. William Shakespeare is arguably the greatest writer of all time. He has a mediocre 3.7 average on Goodreads.

8. Don't spend your life worrying about what you are missing out on. Not to be Buddhist about it – okay, to be a little Buddhist about it – life isn't about being pleased with what you are doing, but about what you are being.

9. Never delay a meal, or sleep, for the sake of the internet.

10. Stay human. Resist the algorithms. Don't be steered towards being a caricature of yourself. Switch off the pop-up ads. Step out of your echo chamber. Don't let anonymity turn you into someone you would be ashamed to be offline. Be a mystery, not a demographic. Be someone a computer could never quite know. Keep empathy alive. Break patterns. Resist robotic tendencies. Stay human.

Never let go

OF THE CHALLENGES we face over the next century, as we begin to merge in more and more complex ways with technology, one of the most interesting might be this: how do we stay human in a digital landscape? How do we keep hold of ourselves and never let go?

Be careful who you pretend to be

KURT VONNEGUT SAID, decades before anyone had an Instagram account, that 'we are what we pretend to be, so we must be careful who we pretend to be'. This seems especially true for the social media age. We have always presented ourselves to the world – chosen which band T-shirt to wear and which words to say and which body parts to shave – but on social media the act of presenting is heightened a stage further. We are eternally one step removed from our online selves. We become walking merchandise. Our profiles are *Star Wars* figures of ourselves.

A picture of a pipe is not a pipe, as Magritte told us. There is a permanent gap between the signifier and the thing signified. An online profile of your best friend is not your best friend. A status update about a day in the park is not a day in the park. And the desire to tell the world about how happy you are, is not how happy you are.

How to be happy

1. Do not compare yourself to other people.
2. Do not compare yourself to other people.
3. Do not compare yourself to other people.
4. Do not compare yourself to other people.
5. Do not compare yourself to other people.
6. Do not compare yourself to other people.
7. Do not compare yourself to other people.

One more click

IF A RAT presses a lever and gets a treat every time, it will keep pressing. But not as often as the rat who presses the lever and gets mixed results – sometimes a treat, sometimes nothing at all.

I used to think social media was harmless. I used to think I was on it because I enjoyed it. But then I was still on it even when I wasn't enjoying it. I remembered that feeling. It was the feeling you get at three in the morning in a bar after your friends have gone home.

Algorithms eat empathy

NOW, THANKS TO clever algorithms, when we do our shopping we are presented with lots of other things that we might like. Things that *people like us* would buy.

If we are on Spotify or YouTube listening to music, they present us with a list of music that is almost exactly like the music we are already listening to.

If we are on Amazon, we are shown the books that people who bought this book also bought.

If we are on social media, we are told to follow more people like the people we already follow. More like us.

We are encouraged to stay in our zone and play it safe, because the internet companies know that on average most people generally like to listen and read and watch and eat and wear the kind of stuff they have already listened to and read and watched and eaten and worn. But all through history we weren't able to do that. We had to go out and compromise and deal with people who weren't like us. With things that weren't like the things we liked. And it was *horrid*.

But now it might be *even worse*.

Now we might end up utterly hating anyone who doesn't think like us. Politicians might end up never trying to reach out to the other side. Difference becomes something to fear, and sneer at, not celebrate. People with similar views end up falling out, unable to stomach even the slightest difference of opinion, until they are trapped in a little echo chamber of one, reading a million versions of the same book, listening to the same song, and retweeting their own opinions until the end of time.

But we are humans. We can resist this. We can resist being confined to a little digital tribe. We can embrace life at its full bandwidth. We are finding ways to do so all the time. Yes, we might be a mess. But our strength *is* our messiness. We don't do things simply because they make sense. The internet can be our ally, not our enemy, in this. The internet contains a whole world. The internet can be what we want it to be. The internet can lead us anywhere we choose. We just have to make sure that we – not the technology, not the designers and engineers able to manipulate our every mood – are the ones doing the choosing.

What people on social media think of social media

IN MY QUEST to insulate my mind from the nervous planet I began to imagine what I would feel like if I abandoned social media altogether. So, while imagining what life would be like without social media I, um, went to social media to try to find out. I decided to ask some of my Twitter followers a big, simple question: 'Is social media good or bad for your mental wellbeing?' The question hit a nerve. I received over 2,000 answers. They offer, of course, a complicated picture. Although, considering that these are people who are active and regular users of social media, the picture is quite negative. I mean, if you imagine asking regular book readers or cinemagoers or horse riders or hill walkers the same thing, it would be unlikely you would get such a mixed response. Anyway, here is a representative selection:

April Joy @AprilWaterson
It's both a coping mechanism and a cause for anxiety. When I've been anxious it's nice to mindlessly scroll and

read for distraction. But at the same time, the incessant need to post things that are 100% guaranteed to be judged by people isn't exactly a calming thought.

Dean Smith @deansmith7
Bad. I can find myself comparing my behind-the-scenes footage (loneliness, anxiety etc) to people's highlights reel (socialising, success etc). I know it's not a true reflection of their lives but it can still get to me.

Miss R! @Fabteachertips
I find when I'm feeling at my lowest, I can easily lose hours to scrolling through my social media feeds in bed alone. I really don't know why I do it, there are so many more productive things I could be doing. It doesn't make me feel better, that's for sure!

Immi Wright @immi_wright
I quit Facebook after I reached v suicidal levels . . . and found I started to feel more confident in myself. I guess FB often presents people's ideal self. On Twitter I just follow rock stars and @dog_rates, so there's far less of that to worry about.

Kieran Sangha @kieran_sangha
It's good in the sense you can connect with others that understand what you're going through. The downside is that it feeds an addiction, like substance abuse, and it can have the power to take over your life.

Hayley Murphy @hayleym_swvegan
Good. There's no one, and I mean NO ONE who understands me in 'real life'. It's literally life-saving to know I'm not alone. Any tool used in the wrong way can be dangerous, but used in the right way it can be incredible.

Bonnie Burton @bonniegrrl
Mixed. Good because I can connect easily with people who inspire me & whom I admire. Bad because social media ends up being a platform for harassment because there are no consequences for horrible behaviour.

Shylah Ellis @MsEels
As a kid, without social media, I basically assumed I was the only person out there suffering from depression. I felt isolated all the time and the only people I had contact with were toxic. Social media has allowed me to interact with incredible people from all over the world.

Kyle Murray @TheKyleMurray

I work in social media and while I think it has some positives, I think if I could keep up with distant friends in other ways, I'd probably just avoid it altogether. It's been weaponized by awful people. I've had FB since 2004 and mostly for nostalgia factor I keep it live.

James @james_____s

A quote I heard recently: 'Facebook is where everyone lies to their friends. Twitter is where they tell the truth to strangers.'

Abigail Rieley @abigailrieley

Both. I've made real friends online & the support if you reach out can be very real BUT if you're down & feeling useless it can be a window into a world you're locked out of, isolating.

Kate Leaver @kateileaver

Mixed, but better than its reputation would suggest. Believe legit friendship can be conducted via social media, which is helpful if you can't leave the house. Getting to glimpse other lives when you're lonely/depressed is helpful at times.

Jayne Hardy @JayneHardy_
Both, I have to have good boundaries around it but when I manage and assert those boundaries, social media is a positive for me.

Gareth L Powell @garethlpowell
As a self-employed writer, Twitter is like my office water cooler. It's where I go to talk to friends and colleagues. Without it, I would feel very isolated.

Claire Allan @ClaireAllan
Mixed. As a writer working alone it gives me social interaction which is sanity saving. But I think it spotlights the best & more frequently the worst of humanity so that increases my anxiety.

Yassmin Abdel-Magied @yassmin_a
It's like anything. It can be great, but needs to be managed well in order for the good to outweigh the bad. Some of my best new friends I've connected with on Twitter.

Hollie Newton @HollieNuisance
I like the ideas and the news and the colourful pictures. I like seeing what my friends are up to. Interacting. But

spend more than a few minutes . . . And I start to feel, increasingly, like an inadequate nobody.

Cole Moreton @colemoreton
Not good. It agitates me, draws me into its angry argument, then I get repulsed and want to shut it all down. Then the cycle starts again.

Rachel Hawkins @ourrachblogs
Mixed. Instagram can leave me feeling jealous. Facebook makes me feel the rage and Twitter sometimes stresses me out.

Kat Brown @katbrown
Both. I get a lot from it (work, laughter, friends, contacts) but I know that my attention span has totally shifted. My focus is very often online. What's about to happen? What COULD have happened? News and dopamine = argh.

Nigel Jay Cooper @nijay
There are times when it feels like being in a room full of people shouting at one another and not listening, so I have to step away from it . . . but there's also the way it connects people, its supportive side and the sense of community. (1/2)

I think the smartphone 'always on' part of the equation is the bigger thing for me. I have to create time when I put the phone down and focus on the real world around me instead of the virtual one. For me, managing that is the key to not being overwhelmed by social. (2/2)

How to be happy (2)

DON'T COMPARE YOUR actual self to a hypothetical self. Don't drown in a sea of 'what if's. Don't clutter your mind by imagining other versions of you, in parallel universes, where you made different decisions. The internet age encourages choice and comparison, but don't do this to yourself. 'Comparison is the thief of joy,' said Theodore Roosevelt. You are you. The past is the past. The only way to make a better life is from inside the present. To focus on regret does nothing but turn that very present into another thing you will wish you did differently. Accept your own reality. Be human enough to make mistakes. Be human enough not to dread the future. Be human enough to be, well, *enough*. Accepting where you are in life makes it so much easier to be happy for other people without feeling terrible about yourself.

7
SHOCK OF THE NEWS

The multiplier effect

IT'S A NERVOUS planet with good reason. The world can be terrifying. Political polarisation, nationalism, the rise of actual Hitler-inspired Nazis, plutocratic elites, terrorism, climate change, governmental upheavals, racism, misogyny, the loss of privacy, ever-cleverer algorithms harvesting our personal data to gain our money or our votes, the rise of artificial intelligence and its implications, the renewed threat of nuclear war, human rights violations, the devastation of the planet. And it's not just *what happens*. After all, the world has always had terrible things happening somewhere. The difference now is that – thanks to camera phones and breaking news and social media and our constant connection to the internet – we *experience* what is happening elsewhere in a more direct and visceral and intimate way than ever before. The experience is multiplied, and leaks out, from a thousand different angles.

Imagine, for instance, if there had been social media and camera phones during the Second World War. If people had seen, in full colour, on smartphones, the consequences of every bomb, or the reality of every concentration camp, or the bloodied and mutilated bodies of soldiers, then the collective psychological experience would have expanded the horror far beyond those who were experiencing it first-hand.

We would do well to remember that this feeling we have these days – that each year is worse than the one previously – is partly just that: a feeling. We are increasingly plugged in to the ongoing travesties and horrors of world news and so the effect is depressing. It's a global sinking feeling. And the real worry is that all the increased fears we feel in themselves risk making the world worse.

If we see footage of a terrorist attack happening it becomes far easier to imagine another one happening, at any time, wherever we live. It doesn't matter if, rationally, we know that we are far more likely to die from cancer or suicide or a traffic accident, the sensational terror we have seen on the news becomes the one that dominates our thoughts. And politicians exploit this, and ramp up the fears and create more division. Which leads to more instability and more opportunities for terrorists to do what they set out to do: cause terror. And then the politicians or political agitators ramp up the fear even higher.

It is like someone who is ill with a compulsive disorder continually underlining their fears – staying indoors, or washing their hands 200 times a day. They are actually doing more to hurt themselves, in the name of protecting themselves. But this time the disorder isn't individual. It is social. It is global.

Shocks to the system

THE WORD 'SHOCK' crops up increasingly among political commentators on TV. You watch/read/scroll the news in the 21st century and it feels like a continual barrage of it. Of shock.

'Oh crap, what now?' That becomes the general reaction.

You click on your favourite news site in the morning and flinch.

Shock may be an unpleasant thing for an individual or a society to experience, but it can be a useful political tool. Ask anyone who has ever had a full-blown panic attack and they will tell you that it makes you think about nothing else but the fear. If you are shocked you are confused. You aren't thinking straight. You become passive. You go where the people tell you to go.

Naomi Klein coined the term the 'shock doctrine' to describe the cynical tactic of systematically using 'the public's disorientation following a collective shock' for corporate or political gain. Oil companies exploiting the shock of war to make inroads into a new country, for instance, or an American president exploiting terrorism to push hard-line anti-immigration measures.

'We don't go into a state of shock when something big and bad happens,' she says. 'It has to be something big and bad *that we do not yet understand.*'

And the trouble is that now we have 24-hour news coverage, where events are continuously breaking but rarely absorbed. We are in a world of news, which by its very nature skims the new moment, garnished with headlines and sound bites, rarely giving us a calmer, more reflective understanding of the big picture.

Shock results in negative but understandable emotions. Fear, sadness, impotence, anger. The temptation to spend our lives tweeting rage at the injustices of the world is a human one, but it isn't enough. Ultimately, it may simply be adding more wails to the collective wails of shock which aid those in power, or on the political extremes, who might want us distracted.

When an individual goes through panic disorder, the main response – amid the terror – is to feel cross and utterly fed up. But there comes a point where, in the process of recovery, you have to reach some kind of understanding and acceptance. Not because it isn't that bad. But precisely because it is *that bad*.

I remember once, during depression, staring up at a clear sky of stars. The wonder of the universe.

At the bottom of the pit, I always had to force myself to find the beauty, the goodness, the love, however hard it was. It was hard to do. But I had to try. Change doesn't just happen by focusing on the place you want to escape. It happens by focusing on where you want to reach. Boost the good guys, don't just knock the bad guys. Find the hope that is already here and help it grow.

Imagine

IMAGINE IF WE had a day where we called human beings human beings. Not nationalities first. Not the religion they follow. Not British. Not American. Not French. Not German. Not Iranian. Not Chinese. Not Muslim. Not Sikh. Not Christian. Not Asian. Not black. Not white. Not man. Not woman. Not CEO of Coca-Cola. Not gang member. Not mother-of-three. Not historian. Not economist. Not BBC journalist. Not Twitter user. Not consumer. Not *Star Trek* fan. Not author. Not aged 17. Or 39. Or 83. Not conservative. Not liberal. Change it all to human. The way we see all turtles as turtles. Human, human, human. Make ourselves see what we pretend to know. Remind ourselves that we are an animal united as a species existing on this tender blue speck in space, the only planet that we know of containing life. Bathe in the corny sentimental miracle of that. Define ourselves by the freakish luck of not only being alive, but being aware of that. That we are here, right now, on the most beautiful planet we'll ever know. A planet where we can breathe and live and fall in love and eat peanut butter on toast and say hello to dogs and dance to music and read *Bonjour Tristesse* and binge-watch TV dramas and notice the sunlight accentuated by hard shadow on a building and feel the wind and the rain on our tender skin and look after each other and lose ourselves in daydreams and night dreams and dissolve into the sweet mystery of ourselves. A day where we are, essentially, precisely as human as each other.

Six ways to keep up with the news and not lose your mind

1. Remember that how you react to the news isn't just about what the news is, but how you get it. The internet and breaking news channels report news in ways that make us feel disorientated. It is easy to believe things are getting worse, when they might just make us *feel* worse. The medium isn't just the message, it's the emotional intensity of that message.

2. Limit the amount of times you look at the news. As my Facebook friend Debra Morse recently commented: 'Remember that in 1973 we typically got our news twice a day: morning paper and evening TV broadcast. And we still got rid of Nixon.'

3. Realise the world is not as violent as it feels. Many writers on this subject – such as the famed cognitive psychologist Steven Pinker – have pointed out that, despite all its horrors, society is less violent than it used to be. 'There is definitely still violence,' says the historian Yuval Noah Harari. 'I live in the Middle

East so I know this perfectly well. But, comparatively, there is less violence than ever before in history. Today more people die from eating too much than from human violence, which is really an amazing achievement.'

4. Be near animals. Non-human animals are therapeutic for all kinds of reasons. One reason is that they don't have news. Dogs and cats and goldfish and antelope literally don't care. The things that are important to us – politics and economics and all of those fluctuating things – are not important to them. And their lives, like ours, still go on. As A.A. Milne wrote in *Winnie-the-Pooh*: 'Some people talk to animals. Not many listen though. That's the problem.'

5. Don't worry about things you can't control. The news is full of things you can't do anything about. Do the things you can do stuff about – raise awareness of issues that concern you, give whatever you can to whichever cause you feel passionate about, and also accept the things you *can't do*.

6. Remember, looking at bad news doesn't mean good news isn't happening. It's happening everywhere. It's happening right now. Around the world. In hospitals, at weddings, in schools and offices and maternity wards,

at airport arrival gates, in bedrooms, in inboxes, out in the street, in the kind smile of a stranger. A billion unseen wonders of everyday life.

In praise of positivity

THE OLD ME, before I ever became ill, was cynical about positivity, about happy songs and pink sunsets and optimistic words of hope. But when I was ill – when I was in the thick of it – my life depended on abandoning that pessimistic side of myself. Cynicism was a luxury for the non-suicidal. I had to find hope. *The thing with feathers*. My life depended on it.

It might seem a stretch to tie psychological healing with social and political healing, but if the personal is political, the psychological is, too. The current political climate seems to be one of division – a division partly fuelled by the internet.

We need to rediscover our commonality as human beings. How does that happen? Well, an alien invasion would be one way, but we can't rely on that.

The problem of politics is the problem of tribes. 'When you separate yourself by belief, by nationality, by tradition, it breeds violence,' taught the philosopher Jiddu Krishnamurti.

One thing mental illness taught me is that progress is a matter of acceptance. Only by accepting a situation can you change it. You have to learn not to be shocked by the shock. Not to be in a state of panic about the panic. To change what you can change and not get frustrated by what you can't.

There is no panacea, or utopia, there is just love and kindness and trying, amid the chaos, to make things better where we can. And to keep our minds wide, wide open in a world that often wants to close them.

8

A SMALL SECTION ON SLEEP

The war on sleep

BEFORE 1879, WHEN Thomas Edison came up with the first practical incandescent light bulb, all lighting had been fuelled by gas and oil. The light bulb, heavily promoted via the Edison & Swan United Electric Light Company, literally set the world alight. The bulbs were practical – small and cheap and safe – and emitted just the right amount of light, and began to take off in homes and businesses throughout the world.

Human beings had, finally, conquered the night. The dark – the source of so many of our primal fears – could now be negated at the flick of a switch. And now, as our evenings could stay lighter for longer, people increasingly started going to bed later. This didn't worry Edison at all. Indeed, he saw it as an unequivocally good thing. In 1914, Edison, by now a living global icon, declared that 'there is really no reason why men should go to bed at all'. He went further: he actually believed sleep was bad for you, and too much was likely to make you lazy. He believed the light bulb was a kind of medicine, and that artificial light could cure 'unhealthy and inefficient' people.

Of course, he was wrong. Without sleep we don't function properly.

Humans, like birds and sea turtles, have body clocks. They – we – have circadian rhythms. That is to say, our bodies react differently at different times of the day. They have evolved to function differently at daytime and nighttime. In another 150,000 generations humans might evolve and adapt to unnatural light, but right now our bodies and minds are still the same bodies and minds of those humans who existed before Edison patented his light bulb. In other words: we need our sleep.

And yet we aren't really getting what we need. The World Health Organization – which has declared a sleep loss epidemic in industrialised nations – recommends we sleep between seven and nine hours a night. But not that many of us do. According to research from the American National Sleep Foundation average American, British and Japanese people all sleep well under seven hours a night while other countries – such as Germany and Canada – hover precariously at the seven-hour mark. And according to more research – this time from Gallup – the average person sleeps for an hour less than they did in 1942.

However, artificial light isn't the only contributing factor here. Sleep experts point to things like the way we work nowadays as well as a growth in loneliness and anxiety that increases our desire to stay up chatting or distract ourselves with entertainment in a frantic 24/7 world.

There are so many incentives to stay awake. So many emails to answer. So many more episodes of our favourite TV show to sit through. So much online shopping to do. Or eBay auctions to monitor. So much news to catch up on. So many social media accounts to update, or concerts to go to, or books to read, or potential dates to chat to, or ambitions to fulfil. So many people – unknown disciples of Edison – wanting us to stay awake.

We all know we tend to be more sad and worried and irritable and lethargic when we haven't slept. Sleep is essential for our wellbeing. When we don't sleep well, it can have serious consequences on our physical and mental state. While some effects of sleeping badly are debatable, there are some on which the medical community have a broad consensus. For instance, according to numerous overlapping studies and sources, not sleeping well:

– Runs down your immune system
– Increases your risk of coronary heart disease

- Increases your risk of stroke
- Increases your risk of diabetes
- Increases your risk of having a car accident
- Is associated with higher rates of breast cancer, colorectal cancer and prostate cancer
- Impairs your ability to concentrate
- Interferes with your memory
- Increases your risk of getting Alzheimer's
- Makes weight gain more likely
- Reduces sex drive
- Increases levels of the stress hormone cortisol
- Increases the likelihood of depression

As University of California 'sleep scientist' Matthew Walker writes in his book *Why We Sleep*: 'there does not seem to be one major organ within the body, or process within the brain, that isn't optimally enhanced by sleep . . . The physical and mental impairments caused by one night of bad sleep dwarf those caused by an equivalent absence of food or exercise.'

Sleep is essential, and amazing. And yet, sleep has traditionally been an enemy of consumerism. We can't shop in our sleep. We can't work or earn or post to Instagram in our sleep. Very few companies – beyond bed manufacturers and duvet sellers and makers of black-out blinds – have actually made money from our sleep. No one has found a way to build a shopping mall that we can enter via our slumber, where advertisers can pay for space in our dreams, where we can spend money while we are unconscious.

Slowly, sleep is becoming a little more commercialised. Now, there are private sleep clinics and sleep centres where people pay for advice on getting a better sleep routine. There are 'sleep trackers', which monitor movement and have been criticised (for instance in a 2018 *Guardian* article on 'clean sleeping') for being unreliable and counter-productive, as they only serve to make people more anxious about sleep.

But largely, sleep remains a sacred space, away from distraction. Which is why seemingly no one can go to bed early.

And now, at this later stage of capitalism, sleep has become seen not just as something that slows work down, but as an actual business rival.

The chief executive of Netflix, Reed Hastings, believes that sleep – not HBO, not Amazon, not any other streaming service – is his company's main competitor. 'You know, think about it,' he said at an industry summit in Los Angeles back in November 2017, cited in *Fast Company*.

'When you watch a show from Netflix and you get addicted to it, you stay up late at night . . . we're competing with sleep, on the margin. And so, it's a very large pool of time.'

So this is the attitude to sleep: something to be suspicious of because it is a time when we are not plugged in, consuming, paying. And this is also our attitude to time: something that mustn't be wasted simply by resting, being, sleeping. We are ruled by the clock. By the light bulb. By the glowing smartphone. By the insatiable feeling we are encouraged to have. The feeling of *this is never enough*. Our happiness is just around the corner. A single purchase, or interaction, or click, away. Waiting, glowing, like the light at the end of a tunnel we can never quite reach.

The trouble is that we simply aren't made to live our lives in artificial light. We aren't made for waking to alarm clocks and falling asleep bathed in the blue light of our smartphone. We live in 24-hour societies but not 24-hour bodies.

Something has to give.

How to sleep on a nervous planet

THERE ARE ALL kinds of pay-for or technological solutions out there. From those sleep-tracking devices to light bulbs free of blue light to hypnotherapy to sleep masks. But many of these consumer products seek to increase our anxiety around sleep.

In fact, the best ways are simple. The most consistent expert advice includes getting into a routine, avoiding caffeine and nicotine and too much late night alcohol (I can vouch for all this), exercising early in the day, avoiding late large meals, relaxing before bed, and getting some natural daylight.

Doing ten minutes of (very) light yoga and slow breathing has worked well for me during anxiety patches where sleep has been problematic.

But one of the most effective solutions, if a little boring, is breathtakingly simple. According to Professor Daniel Forger of the University of Michigan, who led a team of researchers looking at sleeping patterns around the world, we are in the midst of a 'global sleep crisis' as society pushes us to stay up later. The answer, as he told the BBC, is not having more lie-ins. It's going to bed a little earlier, as the later people go to bed, the less sleep they get. Whereas what time we wake up in the morning makes surprisingly little difference. But even the act of going to bed a little earlier might require cultural change. 'If you look at countries that are really getting less sleep then I'd spend less time worrying about alarm clocks and more about what people are doing at night – are they having big dinners at 22:00 or expected to go back to the office?'

Another solution is to be disciplined about your phone and laptop use, and try not to be on them in bed, as the blue light negatively affects the sleep hormone melatonin.

Anyway, I've just realised it's now after midnight as I type these words. I better close my laptop. And I'm going to try to fall asleep without even checking my phone.

9
PRIORITIES

A trip to a homeless shelter

EVEN WHEN THE world is not overtly terrifying us, the speed and pace and distraction of modern existence can be a kind of mental assault that is hard to identify. Sometimes life just seems too complicated, too dehumanising, and we lose sight of what matters.

A few months ago I went to a homeless shelter. It was in Kingston upon Thames, an affluent London suburb which many might imagine would be unlikely to have a homeless problem.

I had been invited there to talk about books and mental health. The place – the award-winning Joel Centre – is based around more than just the idea of giving people a bed for the night. Its ethos is 'Helping People to Believe in Themselves'. A volunteer there told me the idea is that 'the people here are lacking more than somewhere to sleep, they are lacking *belonging*. We aim to give them that. The problem is homelessness not houselessness. And when you are homeless you are missing more than just a bedroom.' He added that working there had made him realise what people 'really need in life – away from all the crap'.

So, the people there, alongside a bed and a lockable wardrobe and access to a washing machine and bathroom, also get to sit around a table with other guests and eat a wholesome meal every day. Often the guests help to cook the meal themselves, and they also play an active part in cleaning the shelter and tending the garden and helping in the local community.

The shelter is *theirs*. They are a part of it.

After I spoke about my experience of mental health problems with them I got talking to the man sitting next to me. He was about my age. He looked like he'd been through a lot, mentally and physically, but he was smiling. He said he'd become homeless after his relationship had broken down and he'd fallen into a depression that he'd tried to deny and had then become an alcoholic. He told me that the centre had saved his life. He pointed vaguely to the door and told me that 'out there' life didn't make sense. He got lost in it.

He found the world dehumanising. Here, though, it was the simple things. 'Just talking to people, sitting around the table with people, working for stuff you can see.'

That was the feeling I had of the place. It was like a distillation of the things people need in life. And it strictly edited out the stuff that harmed the guests – the place was very strict about drink and drugs and so on. It had thought hard about what to let in and what to – literally – shut out.

Although most of us are in a better place in life than the guests at the Joel Centre, its ethos is a good one to adopt. And deceptively simple. Accentuating the things that make you feel good, cutting back the things that make you feel bad, and letting people feel truly connected to the world around them.

That is the biggest paradox, I think, about the modern world. We are all connected to each other but we often feel shut out. The increasing overload and complexity of modern life can be isolating.

Added to that is the fact that we don't always know precisely what makes us feel lonely or isolated. It can make it hard to see what the problems are. It's like trying to open an iPhone to fix it yourself. It sometimes feels like society operates like Apple, as if it doesn't want us to get a screwdriver and look inside to see what the problems are for ourselves. But that's what we need to do. Because often identifying a problem, being mindful of it, becomes the solution itself.

Lonely crowds

THE PARADOX OF modern life is this: we have never been more connected and we have never been more alone. The car has replaced the bus. Working from home (or unemployment) has replaced the factory floor and, increasingly, the group office. TV has replaced the music hall. Netflix is becoming the new cinema. Social media the new meeting friends in the pub. Twitter has replaced the water cooler. And individualism has replaced collectivism and community. We have face-to-face conversations less and less, and more interactions with avatars.

Human beings are social creatures. We are, in George Monbiot's words, 'the mammalian bee'. But our hives have fundamentally changed.

I have noticed as the years pass that the number of my virtual friends is rising while the number of friends I see in real life is shrinking.

I have decided to change this. I am making an effort to get out and socialise with friends at least once a week and I am feeling better for it.

I'm not nostalgic about vinyl and compact discs but I am nostalgic about face-to-face contact. Not Facetime contact. Not Skype contact. But actually talking to someone, out in the elements, with nothing but air between you. At home, I am trying to put my laptop down and speak to my kids so they don't grow up feeling they were behind a MacBook Pro in importance. I am trying not to cancel seeing friends out of sheer can't-be-bothered-ness.

And it is an effort. It's so bloody hard. There are days when I'd find it easier to talk North Korea out of its nuclear weapons programme than to talk myself out of checking social media seventeen times before breakfast.

Online socialising is *easy*. It is *weather-proof*. It never requires a taxi or an ironed shirt. And it's sometimes wonderful. It's often wonderful.

But deep, deep down in the subterranean depths of my soul, I realise that the scent-free, artificially illuminated, digitised, divisive, corporate-owned environment can't fulfil all my needs, any more than takeaway meals can replace the sheer pleasure of eating in a lovely restaurant. And I – someone whose anxiety once tipped into agoraphobia – am increasingly forcing myself to spend longer in that messy, windswept thing we sometimes still romantically call the *real world*.

How to be lonely

HAVE YOU EVER heard a parent moan about their kids' need for constant entertainment?

You know. 'When I was young I could sit in the back of the car and stare out the window at clouds and grass for 17 hours and be perfectly happy. Now our little Misha can't go five seconds in the car without watching *Alvin and the Chipmunks 17* or playing game apps or taking selfies of herself as a unicorn . . .'

That sort of thing.

Well, there is an obvious truth to it. The more stimulation we have, the easier it is to feel bored.

And this is another paradox.

In theory, it has never been easier not to be lonely. There is always someone we can talk to online. If we are away from loved ones then we can Skype them. But loneliness is a feeling as much as anything. When I have had depression, I have been lucky enough to have people who love me all around me. But I had never felt more alone.

I think the American writer Edith Wharton was the wisest person ever on loneliness. She believed the cure for it wasn't always to have company, but to find a way to be happy with your *own* company. Not to be antisocial, but not to be scared of your own unaccompanied presence.

She thought the cure to misery was to 'decorate one's inner house so richly that one is content there, glad to welcome anyone who wants to come and stay, but happy all the same when one is inevitably alone'.

10

PHONE FEARS

A therapy session in the year 2049

ROBOT THERAPIST: So, what is the problem?

MY SON: Well, I think it goes back to my parents.

ROBOT THERAPIST: Really?

MY SON: My dad, specifically.

ROBOT THERAPIST: What was the matter with him?

MY SON: He used to be on his phone all the time. I used to feel like he cared about his phone more than me.

ROBOT THERAPIST: I'm sure that's not true. A lot of people from that generation didn't know all the consequences of their phone use. They didn't know how addictive they were. You have to remember, it was all relatively new back then. And everyone else was doing it, too.

MY SON: Well, it gave me issues. I used to think, Why aren't I as interesting to him as his Twitter feed? Why wasn't I as good to look at as the screen of his phone? If only I didn't feel like I had to distract him to get attention. This was in the days before the 2030 revolution, of course.

ROBOT THERAPIST: Hmmm. Where's your father now?

MY SON: Oh, he died in 2027. He was run over by a driverless car while trying to find a funny gif.

ROBOT THERAPIST: How sad. And what have you been doing since then?

MY SON: I invested in a robot dad. I looked into all the hologram options but I wanted a dad I could hug. And I have programmed him never to check his notifications. He's there when I want him.

ROBOT THERAPIST: That is so wonderful to hear.

How to own a smartphone and still be a functioning human being

1. Don't feel you always have to be there. In the not-so-olden days of letters and landlines, contacting someone was slow and unreliable and an effort. In the age of WhatsApp and Messenger it's free and easy and instant. The flipside of this ease is that we are expected to be there. To pick up the phone. To get back to the text. To answer the email. To update our social media. But we can choose not to feel that obligation. We can sometimes just *let them wait*. We can risk our social media getting stale. And if our friends are friends they will understand when we need some headspace. And if they aren't friends, why bother getting back anyway?

2. Turn off notifications. This is essential. This keeps me (just about) sane. All of them. All notifications. You don't need any of them. Take back control.

3. Have times of the day where you're not beside your phone. Okay, I'm bad at this one. But I'm getting better. No one needs their phone all the time. We

don't need it by the bed. We don't need it while we're eating meals at home. We don't need it when we go out for a run. Here's something I do now: I go for a walk without my phone. I know it sounds ridiculous to present that as some big achievement, but for me it was. It's like exercise. It takes effort.

4. Don't press the home button to check the screen every two minutes for texts. Practise feeling the urge to check and don't.

5. Don't tie your anxiety levels to how much power you have left on your phone.

6. Don't swear at your phone. Don't plead with your phone. Don't bargain with your phone. Don't throw your phone across the room. It is indifferent to your feelings. If the phone has no signal, or no power, it is not because it hates you. It is because it is an inanimate object. It is, in short, a phone.

7. Don't put your phone by the bed. I'm not judging, by the way. Most people sleep with their phone by the bed because they've replaced alarm clocks. Most nights I have the phone by the bed. My parents have their phones by the bed. Everyone I know has their phones by their beds. Maybe one day our beds will *be* our phones. But I do seem to sleep better when my phone

isn't by my bed. You know, if it's in another room, or even just another part of the room. I know it might be unrealistic. But it's good to have an aspiration. A dream to work towards. To fantasise about the day when we're strong enough never to need to have the phone by our beds. Like the olden days. The 1800s. The 1900s. 2006.

8. Practise app minimalism. An overload of apps and options adds to the choice but also stress of phone use. We are given an almost infinite array of things we can add to our phones. But more choice leads to more decisions and more stress. You were born without any apps on your phone. Hey! Guess what? You were born without any phone at all. And life was still beautiful.

9. Don't try to multitask. We have phones that can do everything from map read to tune our guitars, and it's tempting to imagine that we can do as many things, and all at once. For instance, while writing this one point alone I have had to consciously stop myself from checking my emails, checking my text messages, checking my social media. It took effort. According to neuroscientist Daniel Levitin, we aren't really made for the kind of multitasking the internet age

encourages us to do. 'Even though we think we're getting a lot done, ironically, multitasking makes us demonstrably less efficient,' he writes, in *The Organized Mind: Thinking Straight in the Age of Information Overload*. Multitasking creates a dopamine-addiction cycle, rewarding the brain for losing focus. It can also increase stress and lower IQ. 'Instead of reaping the big rewards that come from sustained, focused effort, we instead reap empty rewards from completing a thousand little sugar-coated tasks,' concludes Levitin.

10. Accept uncertainty. The temptation to check your phone is down to uncertainty. That's what makes it so addictive. You want someone to get back to your text but you don't know if they have. You want to check. You want to see the promise and mystery of the three little circles, dancing with hope. You want to know how your photo or status update is going down. But why do we need to know right now? Why can't it all wait till after your lie-in/meeting/walk/TV show/ meal/daydream? Do people really need to check their phones during meetings, or while attending funerals? Maybe if we understood that the checking is never fully satisfying we wouldn't. Because there is no end to the uncertainty. There is no final checking of your

phone. Think of all the times you checked your phone yesterday. Did you *really* need to so often? I certainly didn't. I have definitely cut down, but still have a way to go. How many times do you touch your phone a day? Or look at it? It might be hard to keep count. The answer might be well in the hundreds. Imagine, I say to myself, if you just looked at your phone, say, five times a day. What catastrophe would occur?

Glow

I USED TO be obsessed with glowing windows and street-lamps when I was a kid. From the back of the car I would stare out and look at windows glowing pink through red curtains, like ET's chest, and wonder about the life going on inside. There is something about the glow of artificial light that I find mesmerising. When I was eight years old – in 1983 – my parents had an old AA travel guide called *Discover America* and it had a double image of the Las Vegas Strip as seen at night. 'I want to go *there*,' I announced to my mum, to her distaste. She never took me.

'It's late,' I say to Andrea.

We read a little, then switch the lights off, always later than we should. Every time, I imagine the square light of our window turning black, to anyone walking by outside.

'Night,' Andrea says.

'Night.'

It will be some time after midnight and the room will be dark except for the glow of a phone.

'Matt, are you going to go to sleep?'

'I tried. My mind's racing.'

'You should put the phone down.'

'It's just my tinnitus is bad. This distracts me.'

'Well, it's stopping me going to sleep.'

'Okay, sorry. I'm putting the phone down.'

'You know what'll happen if you have too many bad nights.'

'I know. Night . . .'

And I close my eyes, and my mind still races with a thousand worries, attracting attention like illuminated signs in Vegas, tainting my dreams and waiting to dissolve in daylight.

How to get out of bed

1. Wake up.
2. Pick up phone.
3. Stare at phone for 72 minutes.
4. Sigh.
5. Get out of bed.

Alternatively, once in a while, try skipping stages two to four.

A problem in your pocket

WHILE WRITING THIS book, early in 2018, I was asked by *The Observer* to contribute to an article where lots of writers asked the novelist and essayist Zadie Smith questions. I took the opportunity, not least because I had seen Zadie Smith at a couple of literary parties when I was newly published and had been crippled and mute with anxiety and hadn't dared to go over and talk to her.

I had read about her social media scepticism and how she values her 'right to be wrong', and so I asked her, 'Do you worry about what social media is doing to society?'

She didn't mince her words, and started with a critique of smartphones.

'I can't stand the phones and don't want them in my life in any form. They make me feel anxious, depressed, dead inside, unhinged. But I fully support anyone who finds them delightful and a profound asset to their existence.'

Although a self-described 'Luddite abstainer', Smith does think the time is right to look at how we're using this technology. 'What is this little device in your pocket doing to your intimate relationships with others?' she asked. 'To your behaviour as a citizen within a society? Maybe nothing! Maybe it's all totally cool. But maybe not? . . . Do we need it resting by our pillows at night? Do our seven-year-olds need phones? Do we wish to pass down our own dependency and obsession? It all has to be thought through. We can't just let the tech companies decide for us.'

I use my phone a lot more than Smith does but despite that – or maybe because of it – I share a lot of her anxieties. And there are signs that even those working for the tech companies are concerned, which means we should be even more worried about where those stupendously powerful companies are leading us. For instance, it's been known – at least since *The New York Times* reported it in 2011 – that many Apple and Yahoo! employees choose to send their kids to schools which shun technology, such as the Waldorf School of the Peninsula in Los Altos.

There are also many tech insiders who have come out to warn against the things they have had a hand in creating. There was the guy who invented the 'Like' button on Facebook, Justin Rosenstein, who has said that technology is so addictive his phone has a parent-control feature to stop him downloading apps and restrict his use of social media. And, as a side point, it is worth mentioning that the Facebook 'like' function is also what helps the data miners understand who we are. Our online likes reveal everything from our sexual orientation to our politics, and can be harvested to better influence us, as seen in the Cambridge Analytica scandal in 2018, where reports suggested 50 million Facebook members had their data improperly accessed by the British firm that helps businesses and political groups 'change audience behaviour'.

'It is very common,' Rosenstein told *The Guardian* in 2017, like a latter-day Dr Frankenstein, 'for humans to develop things with the best of intentions and for them to have unintended, negative consequences . . . Everyone is distracted, all the time.'

And two of Twitter's founders have expressed similar regrets. Ev Williams – who stepped down as CEO in 2010 – told *The New York Times* in 2017 that he was unhappy with the way Twitter had helped Donald Trump become president. 'It's a very bad thing, Twitter's role in that.'

Another Twitter co-founder Biz Stone has other regrets. He stated in an interview with Inc. that he thought the big wrong turn Twitter made was when it allowed strangers to tag people in their posts, as it created an environment rife for bullying. Another employee, according to Buzzfeed, has called Twitter a 'honeypot for assholes'.

And, in early 2018, Tim Cook – CEO of Apple – declared to a group of students in Essex, England, that he doesn't think children (such as his nephew) should use a social network, or overuse technology at all, which shows that these aren't simply 'Luddite' concerns.

Indeed, a group of former tech employees have gone further, and set up the Center for Humane Technology, aimed at 'realigning technology with humanity's best interests' and reversing the 'digital attention crisis'.

Now, at long last, there are many instances of tech people getting together to discuss concerns. For instance, at a 2018 conference in Washington called Truth About Tech, speakers included Google's former 'ethicist' and now prominent tech whistleblower Tristan Harris and early investor of Facebook Roger McNamee, along with politicians and members of lobby groups such as Common Sense Media, who are trying to combat tech addiction in young people. A variety of concerns were raised, such as the way Google's Gmail 'hijacks' minds, or how Snapchat exploits teenage friendships to fuel tech addiction via functions like 'Snapchat streaks' where users can see how many interactions they've had with friends per day. According to *The Guardian*, Harris compared the tech world to the Wild West in that the ethos is 'build a casino wherever you want' and McNamee compared it to the tobacco and food industries in the past, where cigarettes were promoted as healthy, or where manufacturers of ready meals failed to mention their products were loaded with salt. The difference being that with, say, an addiction to cigarettes, is that the cigarettes had no information about us. They didn't collect our data. They couldn't know us better than our own families. The internet, of course, can know everything about us. It can know who our friends are, it can know our taste in music, it can know our health concerns, our love life, and our politics – and internet companies can keep using this information to make their products ever more addictive. And at the moment, warn the tech insiders, there isn't much regulation to stop them.

An increasing amount of research reinforces their concerns. For example, studies that show how technology contributes to a state of 'continual partial attention' and how it can be addictive. One 2017 study from the McCombs School of Business at the University of Texas concluded that the mere presence of your smartphone can reduce 'cognitive capacity'.

At the time of writing, there is still no official recognition that 'smartphone addiction' or 'social media addiction' are psychological disorders, although the fact that the World Health Organization now classifies video game addiction as an official mental disorder suggests that there is a growing understanding of how seriously technology can affect our mental health. But that understanding still has a long way to go, and clearly lags behind the disorientating speed of technological change.

Though pressure is rising. In 2018, for instance, CNN reported that the mighty Unilever threatened to pull its advertising from Facebook and Google unless they combat toxic problems – including privacy concerns, objectionable content and a lack of protections for children – which are 'eroding social trust, harming users and undermining democracies'. There is a growing awareness that the great power of internet companies must come, Spiderman-style, with a great sense of responsibility. However, it is debatable as to how much responsibility they will develop without real social and financial pressure of the kind we are only beginning to see. As with fast food or cigarettes or the gun industry, the companies making a profit from something might be the most reluctant to see the potential problems. So when the people on the inside are among those raising the alarm, we should really listen.

II

THE DETECTIVE
OF DESPAIR

'These fragments I have shored against my ruins'

—T.S. Eliot, *The Waste Land*

Awareness

WHEN I FIRST became ill, at the age of 24 – when I 'broke down' – the world became sharper. Painfully so. Shadows had sudden weight, clouds became greyer, music became louder. I became more alert to everything I had been numb to. I noticed the things that made me feel worse about the modern world. Things that probably make many of us feel worse. I felt the wearying pressure of advertising, the frantic madness of crowds and traffic, the suffocating nature of social expectation.

Illness has a lot to teach wellness.

But when I am well I forget these things. The trick is to keep hold of that knowledge. To turn recovery into prevention. To live how I live when I am ill, without being ill.

Hope

THERE ARE SOME factors affecting our mental health that are genetic, and down to an individual's wiring or brain chemistry. But we can't do much about the things handed down to us in our genetic code. What is more interesting are the transient aspects, the triggers that change with time and societies. These are the things we can do stuff about.

Other eras have had their own particular mental health crises of course. But the fact that every age has struggled with its own particular problems should not make us complacent about our own culture.

And the great thing about this – the liberating thing – is that if our anxiety is in part a product of culture, it can also be *something we can change by changing our reaction to that culture*. In fact, we don't even need to consciously change at all. The change can happen simply by being aware.

When it comes to our minds, awareness is very often the solution itself.

The detective of despair

I THINK THE world is always going to be a mess. And I am always going to be a mess. Maybe you're a mess, too. But – and this bit is everything for me – I believe it's possible to be a happy mess. Or, at least, a less miserable mess. A mess who can *cope*.

'In all chaos there is a cosmos,' said Carl Jung, 'in all disorder a secret order.'

Mess is actually okay. As you will be aware by now, I am trying to write about the messiness of the world and the messiness of minds by writing a deliberately messy book. That's my excuse, anyway. Fragments that I hope together make a kind of whole. I hope it all *makes sense*. Or if it doesn't make sense, I hope it makes nonsense in ways that might get you thinking.

The problem is not that the world is a mess, but that we expect it to be otherwise. We are given the idea that we have control. That we can go anywhere and be anything. That, because of free will in a world of choice, we should be able to choose not just where to go online or what to watch on TV or which recipe to follow of the billion online recipes, but also what to feel. And so when we don't feel what we want or expect to feel, it becomes confusing and disheartening. Why can't I be happy when I have so much choice? And why do I feel sad and worried when I don't really have anything to be sad and worried about?

And the truth is that when I first became ill, at the very beginning, I didn't even know what I had, let alone what might be triggering it. I had no understanding of the hell I wanted to escape, I just wanted to escape it. If your leg is on fire you don't know the temperature of the flames. You just know that you're in pain.

Later, doctors would offer labels. 'Panic disorder', 'generalised anxiety disorder' and 'depression'. These labels were worrying, but also important, because they gave me something to work with. They stopped me feeling like an alien. I was a human being with human illnesses, which other humans have had – millions and millions of humans – and most of them had either overcome their illnesses or had somehow managed to live with them.

Even after I knew the names of the illnesses I had, I believed they were all stemming from inside me. They were just *there*, the way the Grand Canyon was just there, a fixed feature of my psychic geography which I could do nothing about.

I would never be able to enjoy music again. Or food. Or books. Or conversation. Or sunlight. Or cinema. Or a holiday. Or anything. I was rotten now, to my core, like a, like a, like a (there are never enough metaphors for depression), like a diseased tree. A diseased tree whose girlfriend and parents say, over and over, 'You'll get better. We'll find a way and we will get you better.'

And, of course, there were different remedies. I tried the diazepam a doctor gave me. I tried the various tinctures a homeopath gave me. I tried the recommendations of friends and family. I tried St John's Wort and lavender oil. I tried sleeping pills. I tried talking to telephone helplines. Then I stopped trying. I had a nightmarish time on diazepam and an even more nightmarish time coming off diazepam. I should probably have tried taking different pills, but – judge me if you will – I didn't. I wasn't thinking rationally. Complicating the situation was the fact that I was scared – I mean, terrified beyond anything I'd ever known – of trying more pills, or of seeking more help now that nothing had worked.

When I mentioned this in *Reasons to Stay Alive* a couple of people thought I was making a statement against pills, so I will say here, as clearly as possible: I am not against pills. Yes, there are all kinds of issues with the pharmaceutical industry and the scientific research is still a work in progress (as scientific research, by its nature, tends to be), but I also know that pills have saved many people's lives. I know of people who say they could not survive without them. I also believe there would be medication out there that could probably have helped me, but I didn't find it. I don't believe pills are a *total* solution. I also believe certain misprescribed pills can make some people feel worse, but that is the same with anything. You could get the wrong pills for arthritis or your heart condition. And to say that pills aren't the only answer is common sense. They rarely are. If you have arthritis, yoga and swimming and hot sunshine might be helpful and pills might also be helpful. It's not an either/or situation. We have to find what works for us. Also, in my case, I was traumatised, and wasn't even close to thinking straight.

At that time, trying things that didn't work only made life worse. As I said, there may well have been the right treatment out there for me – talk or medication – but I wasn't lucky enough to find it. I wasn't brave enough to seek it out. The pain was as much as I could bear to *just about* stay alive. I couldn't risk a gram of difference, that was my logic. Every day felt like life or death. Not because the pain wasn't bad enough to keep going back to the doctor, but because it was too bad. Writing that down, I realise how ridiculous that sounds, but that was my reality then. Everything I had tried to combat the turmoil inside my head had failed. And, to be honest, the doctors I had encountered hadn't been that understanding. I sincerely believe that things have moved on in lots of ways since the turn of this century.

So, anyway, I was there, in this pit, desperately trying to find a way out as every escape route seemed to be closing.

And, as many people in this situation discover, you acquire evidence like a detective trying to solve a murder. At first there were no clues, or none I could see. Every day in that pit was hell. Every day, in those first few weeks and months, contained moments of such heavy emotional pain that they stopped any hope breaking through. But the pain, I started to realise, although internal, often had external triggers. There was nothing I had found that made me feel better. Then I realised that certain things could make me feel worse: drinking alcohol, smoking, loud music, crowds. The world *gets in*. It always gets in, however we are doing. But until I became ill, I never knew how.

Note to self

KEEP CALM. KEEP going. Keep human. Keep pushing. Keep yearning. Keep perfecting. Keep looking out the window. Keep focus. Keep free. Keep ignoring the trolls. Keep ignoring pop-up ads and pop-up thoughts. Keep risking ridicule. Keep curious. Keep hold of the truth. Keep loving. Keep allowing yourself the human privilege of mistakes. Keep a space that is you and put a fence around it. Keep reading. Keep writing. Keep your phone at arm's length. Keep your head when all about you are losing theirs. Keep breathing. Keep inhaling life itself.

Keep remembering where stress can lead.

(Keep remembering that day in the shopping centre.)

Fear and shopping

I WAS IN a shopping centre, crying.

Me, aged 24, surrounded by crowds of people and shops and illuminated signs, unable to cope.

'No,' I whispered, as my breathing lost its rhythm. 'I can't do this.'

'Matt?'

It had been a test. To go with Andrea, then my girl-friend, to this city near her parents' home – Newcastle, in the north of England – and do some shopping. I had no idea what we were shopping *for*. My focus was simply on making it through without having a panic attack.

To be like any other normal person.

'I'm sorry, I just can't, I . . .'

There I was. Pathetic. A young man. In a world that had told me – everywhere from TV shows to the school sports field – that being a man means being *strong* and *tough* and *silent* in the face of pain, a world that showed us that being young was about having fun and being free in the bright, shining land of youth. And here I was, in the supposed prime of my life, *crying about nothing in a shopping centre*. Well, it wasn't really about nothing. It was about pain. And terror. A pain and terror I had never known until a little over a month before, while working in Spain, when I had a panic attack that started and didn't stop and then became fused with a terrible, indescribable sense of dread and malaise and hopelessness which seeped into my flesh and bones.

The despair had been so strong that it had very nearly taken my life. There had seemed no way out. However scary death was, this living terror had seemed worse. Everyone has a limit – a point at which they can't take any more – and, almost out of nowhere, I had reached mine.

'It's all right,' Andrea was saying, holding my hand. More mother or nurse than girlfriend in that moment.

'No, it isn't. I'm sorry. I'm sorry.'

'Did you take the diazepam this morning?'

'Yes, but it's not working.'

'It's going to be all right. It's just panic.'

Just panic.

Her concerned eyes made it worse. I'd already put her through so much. All I had to do was walk. Walk and talk and breathe like a normal human being. It wasn't rocket science. But right then, it might as well have been.

'I can't.'

Andrea's face hardened now. Her jaw clenched and mouth tightened. Even she had limits. She was cross *at* me and *for* me. 'You can do it.'

'No, Andi, I really fucking can't. You don't understand.'

People were looking at us, casting sideways glances in our direction as they walked along weighed down with carrier bags.

'Just breathe. Just breathe slowly.'

I tried to breathe deep, but the air could hardly make it beyond my throat.

'I . . . I . . . I . . . There's no air.'

Earlier in the day, I hadn't been feeling as bad as this. Just a low-level unshiftable despair. On the bus into the city, the fear had crept over me, like being slowly wrapped in an itchy blanket.

Now my whole body was alive with terror.

I was frozen right there, standing outside Vision Express, surrounded by life yet alone. I began to swallow. To try to direct myself. Compulsive swallowing had been one of a few mild OCD symptoms I had developed. This time I was actually wanting that symptom just to distract me from a worse one. But it didn't work.

There was no hope. There was no way out. Life was for other people.

I had held back the world, and now it was caving in. And Andrea's voice became something far away, the last hope, trying to reach the person I no longer was.

You only have one mind

WHEN I LOOK back on the shopping centre experience –
one experience among many similar ones that sometimes
burst into my brain like a Vietnam flashback without
the violence – I try to dissect it. I relive the past in order to
accept it and learn from it. Not just to learn how not to have
panic attacks, but to learn how my mind intersects with the
world and work out how to be less stressed generally.

The first problem was that it took place within my earli-
est experience of anxiety and depression. When you have a
bout of mental illness for the first time, you imagine this is
how your life is going to be for ever. You will have depression punctuated by panic attacks and that is how things
will stay. And that was terrifying. The claustrophobia of it.
There seemed no way out.

The second problem was that I still had no idea how to
deal with panic attacks. That lesson was going to take
years to learn.

And the third problem was that I didn't understand
how the external and the internal were connected. I

didn't know how related 'what you feel' is to 'where you are'. I didn't know that the world of shops and sales and marketing is not always good for minds. A lot of research has been done in the last two years about the effect of external environments on our health. For instance, a 2013 study commissioned by the mental health charity Mind and run by the University of Essex compared the experience of walking in a shopping centre with a 'green walk' around Belhus Woods Country Park in Essex. Although walking is known to be good for a mind – indoors or outdoors – 44 per cent of the people who walked in a shopping centre said they felt a decrease in self-esteem. Whereas nearly all (90 per cent) of the people who went for the forest walk felt their self-esteem increase. There is an increasing amount of research like this, as I'll mention later, about how nature is good for our minds. But at the time I knew none of that. Indeed, most of the research hadn't been done.

It makes sense that shopping centres aren't easy places to be in. A shopping centre is a deliberately stimulating environment, designed not to calm or comfort, but merely to get us to spend money. And as anxiety is often a trigger for consumption, feeling calm and satisfied would probably work against the shopping centre's best interests.

Calmness and satisfaction – in the agenda of the shopping centre – are destinations we reach by *purchasing*. Not places already *there*.

The fourth problem was guilt. I felt guilty about symptoms I didn't really see as symptoms of an illness. I saw them as symptoms of me-ness.

Another lesson I am still coming to understand – and writing this book is helping me – is that distraction didn't and doesn't work. For one thing, shopping centres are deliberately very distracting environments, but they didn't take me out of myself, only into myself. The bustling crowds of other people didn't help connect me to humanity. I felt more alone among masses of people than I did when it was just me and one other person, or even just myself.

This was an already familiar tactic of mine: trying to distract myself from one torment by finding another. Years before Twitter, and the mind-numbing compulsive checking of social media, I had the desperate need for distraction. But it was no good. You develop symptoms more by fighting them than inviting them. Distraction is an attempt to escape that rarely works. You don't put out a fire by ignoring the fire. You have to acknowledge the fire. You can't compulsively swallow or tweet or drink your way out of pain. There comes a point at which you have to face it. To face yourself. In a world of a million distractions you are still left with only one mind.

The mannequins who inflict pain

WHEN I NOW think of that particular panic attack I think of how the world got in. Even at the time I had an instinctive – if not totally conscious – idea of the triggers around me. Even a shop's mannequins added to it.

There I was. In that enclosed and busy and artificial commercial space. Past the point of no return. My own personal singularity. The rational knowledge, as I looked at Andrea, that I was in the all too familiar process of ruining our day.

I closed my eyes to escape the stimulation of the shopping centre and saw nothing but monsters and demons, a mental bank of creatures and images worse than any hydra or cyclops – my own personal underworld that was now only ever a blink or a thought away.

'Come on, you can do it. Breathe slowly.'

I tried to do what she said: to breathe slowly, but the air didn't feel like air. It didn't feel like anything. My *self* didn't feel like anything.

I wiped my eyes.

Opposite Vision Express was a clothes shop. I can't remember which one. But what I can remember, printed with the weight of trauma in my memory, is that there were mannequins in dresses in the window. The kind of mannequins with heads. Heads which were grey and hairless and with features that hinted abstractly at a nose and eyes, but no mouth. The mannequins stood in unnatural angular poses.

They seemed deeply malevolent. As if they were sentient beings who not only knew my pain, but were part of it. Were partly *responsible* for it.

Indeed, this would be a key feature of my anxiety *and* depression over the following months and years. The sense that parts of the world contained a secret external malevolence that could press a despairing weight and pain into you. It could be found in a smiling face on a glossy magazine. It could be found in the devilish red stare of rear tail-lights. Or the too-bright blue glow of a computer screen.

And yes, it could be found in the sinister echo of humanity in a shop mannequin.

One day, when I was ready to face my pain, this feeling of extreme sensitivity would actually help me. It would help me understand that if external things could have a negative impact, then other external things might have a positive impact. But right then I was worried I was losing my mind.

I was convinced I wasn't made for the reality of the world. And in a way, I was right. I wasn't made *for* the world. I was, like everyone, made *by* the world. I was made by parents and culture and TV and books and politics and school and maybe even shopping centres.

So, I either needed a new me. Or a new planet. And I didn't yet know how to find either. Which is why I felt suicidal.

'I've got to get out of here,' I said at the time, wiping my eyes like a toddler lost in a supermarket.

The 'here' was broad enough to mean anything from 'my head' to 'the planet'. More immediately, of course, the 'here' was the shopping centre.

'Okay, okay, okay,' Andrea said. She was right next to me. She was also thousands of miles away. She scanned around for the nearest exit. 'This way.'

We got outside, into natural light. And we went back to Andrea's parents', and I lay on Andrea's childhood bed and told her parents I had a bit of a headache, because a headache was easier for them to understand than this invisible cyclone. Anyway, I felt varying degrees of bad for many weeks and months, but eventually I began to recover. And, even better, to understand.

A wish

I SO WISH I could explain something to my younger self. I wish I could tell myself that it wasn't all *me*. I wish I could say that there were things I could do. Because my anxiety, my depression, wasn't just *there*. Illness, like injury, often has context.

When I fall into a frantic or despairing state of mind, full of unwelcome thoughts that can't slow down, it is often the result of a series, a sequence of things. When I do too much, think too much, absorb too much, eat too badly, sleep too little, work too hard, get too frazzled by life, there it is.

A repetitive strain injury of the mind.

How to exist in the 21st century and not have a panic attack

1. Keep an eye on yourself. Be your own friend. Be your own parent. Be kind to yourself. Check on what you are doing. Do you need to watch the last episode of the series when it is after midnight? Do you need that third or fourth glass of wine? Is that *really* in your best interests?

2. Declutter your mind. Panic is the product of overload. In an overloaded world we need to have a filter. We need to simplify things. We need to disconnect sometimes. We need to stop staring at our phones. To have moments of not thinking about work. A kind of mental feng shui.

3. Listen to calm noise. Things that aren't as stimulating as music. Waves, your own breath, a breeze through the leaves, the purr of a cat, and best of all: *rain*.

4. Let it happen. If you feel panic rising the instinctive reaction is to panic some more. To panic *about* the panic. To meta-panic. The trick is to try to feel panic

without panicking *about* it. This is nearly – but not quite – impossible. I had panic disorder – a condition defined not by the occasional panic attack but by frequent panic attacks and the continuous hellish fear of the next one. By the time I'd had hundreds of panic attacks I began to tell myself I wanted it. I didn't, obviously. But I used to work hard at trying to invite the panic – as a test, to see how I could cope. The more I invited it, the less it wanted to stay around.

5. Accept feelings. And accept that they are just that: feelings.

6. Don't grab life by the throat. 'Life should be touched, not strangled,' said the writer Ray Bradbury.

7. It is okay to release fear. The fear tries to tell you it is necessary, and that it is protecting you. Try to accept it as a feeling, rather than valid information. Bradbury also said: 'Learning to let go should be learned before learning to get.'

8. Be aware of where you are. Are your surroundings over-stimulating? Is there somewhere you can go that is calmer? Is there some nature you can look at? Look up. In city centres, the tops of buildings are less intense than the shop fronts you see at head level. The sky helps, too.

9. Stretch and exercise. Panic is physical as well as mental. For me, running and yoga help more than anything. Yoga, especially. My body tightens, from hours of being hunched over a laptop, and yoga stretches it out again.

10. Breathe. Breathe deep and pure and smooth. Concentrate on it. Breathing is the pace you set your life at. It's the rhythm of the song of you. It's how to get back to the centre of things. The centre of yourself. When the world wants to take you in every other direction. It was the first thing you learned to do. The most essential and simple thing you do. To be aware of breath is to remember you are alive.

12

THE THINKING BODY

Four humours

ONCE UPON A time, in Ancient Greece, doctors explained the human body with reference to the 'four humours'. Every health complaint could be assessed as an excess or deficiency of one of four distinct bodily fluids: black bile, yellow bile, phlegm and blood.

In Roman times, the four humours evolved to correspond with four temperaments. For instance, if you had anger issues, you would be told you had too much yellow bile, the fire humour. Which means when you tell someone to 'chill' you are echoing official health advice from Ancient Rome.

If you were feeling depressed, or melancholic, that was down to an overload of black bile. In fact, the very word 'melancholia' stems via Latin from the ancient Greek words *melas* and *kholé*, which literally meant 'black bile'.

This system seems ludicrously unscientific. But in one way, at least, it was advanced. Namely, it did not make a division between physical and mental health.

The philosopher René Descartes is largely to blame for this distinction. He believed minds and bodies were entirely separate. Back in the 1640s he suggested that the body works like an unthinking machine and that the mind, in contrast, is non-material.

People liked the idea. It was a hit. And it still impacts society.

But this split makes little sense.

Mental health is intricately related to the whole body. And the whole body is intricately related to mental health. You can't draw a line between a body and a mind any more than you can draw a line between oceans.

They are entwined.

Physical exercise is known to have a positive impact on all kinds of mental things, from depression to ADHD. And physical illnesses have mental effects. We can hallucinate with flu. A cancer diagnosis can make us depressed. Asthma can cause us to panic. A heart attack can cause mental trauma. If you have a bad lower back – or tinnitus, or chest pain, or a lowered immune system, or a painful stomach – because of stress, is that a mental or a physical problem?

I feel we need to stop seeing mental and physical health as either/or and more as a both/and situation. There is no difference. We are mental. We are physical. We are not split up into unrelated sections. We are not an existential department store. We are everything at once.

Guts

BRAINS ARE PHYSICAL.

And besides, thoughts aren't just the products of brains. As cognitive scientist Guy Claxton writes in *Intelligence in the Flesh*, 'the body, the gut, the senses, the immune system, the lymphatic system, are so instantaneously and so complicatedly interacting with the brain that we can't draw a line across the neck and say, "above the line it's smart and below the line it's menial". We do not have bodies. We *are* bodies.'

Then there is the issue of the 'little brain' – a network of 100 million neurons (nerve cells) in our stomach and gut. Okay, so it is nowhere near the 85 billion neurons that our 'first brain' has, but it is not to be sniffed at. One hundred million neurons are the amount a cat has in her head.

When we get 'butterflies' in the stomach before a job interview, or when we get hungry before a late lunch, that is our 'second brain' talking to our first brain.

So, in other words, this suggests that the idea of 'mental health' being separate to our physical self is as outdated as Descartes' dodgy wig.

And yet we still suffer from the divide. We separate the world of work into mind jobs and body jobs. 'Skilled' jobs, which need what we generally see as intelligence and a 'good education', and lower-valued 'unskilled' jobs which often tend to be manual labour. White collar and blue collar.

There is an intelligence to movement. An intelligence to dance. An intelligence to playing sport. And yet we casually section people off, from school age, deciding if someone is sporty or academic or – in *Breakfast Club* speak – a 'jock' or a 'brain'. This then determines their career path, whether it will result in a lower-paid manual job or a higher-paid job staring at an Excel spreadsheet. And we divide culture into high and low. Books that make us laugh or give us heart palpitations are seen as less worthy than books that make you 'think'.

The line we draw between minds and bodies makes no sense the more we stare at it, and yet we base our entire system of healthcare on that line. And not just healthcare. Our selves and societies, too. It's time to change this. It's time to rejoin the two parts. It's time to accept our whole human self.

A side note on stigma

WE AREN'T ENCOURAGED to talk about our mental health until we are mentally ill, as if we have to fake being in 100 per cent full health. Stress simply isn't taken seriously enough. Or it is taken so seriously that people are ashamed of talking about their bad mental health days. Either way, this leads to more people becoming not just stressed, but ill.

And when we become ill, and might talk about it, we encounter a new stigma.

Too often, we view mental illness as a product of the person in a way we don't with other illnesses. Because mental illness is seen as intrinsically different, we talk of it in different, more scandalised terms. Think of the words used about mental illness.

Newspapers and magazines sometimes talk about celebrities 'confessing' to depression and anxiety and eating disorders and addictions, as if those things are crimes. And *actual* crimes are too often explained as the product of an illness – mass shootings and sexual abuse are often given the media context of 'mental health problems' or 'addiction' rather than terrorism and sex crimes. In reality, people with mental illness are far more likely to be *victims* of crimes.

We also don't really know how to talk about suicide. When we do talk about it we tend to use that verb – commit – which carries connotations of taboo and criminality, an echo of the days when it *was* criminal. (I have recently been trying to say 'death by suicide' but it still feels a bit forced and false on my tongue.) Many people struggle to deal with the very idea of taking your own life, as it seems a kind of insult to us all, if you see suicide as a choice, because someone has chosen to give up on living, this sacred precious thing, as fragile as a bird's egg. But personally I know that suicide isn't such a clear-cut choice. It can be something you dread and fear but feel compelled towards because of the new pain of living. So, it's uncomfortable, talking about it. But talk we must, because an atmosphere of shame and silence prevents people getting the right help and can make them feel more freakishly lonely. It can, in short, be fatal.

Suicide is the biggest killer of women and men between the ages of 20 and 34. It is also the biggest killer of men under the age of 50 (at least in the country where I live, the UK. Other European countries have similarly bleak statistics. In the US, where firearms contribute to the depressing statistics, suicide is the tenth leading cause of death overall, across all ages and genders, though as with Europe, Canada and Australia, men are over three times more likely to kill themselves than women). These deaths are so often preventable. This is why we must ignore the pleas to 'man up' and find true strength instead. The strength for men and women to speak out.

The echoes of historical shame are everywhere in our words. For another example, when we talk about someone 'battling their demons' we are conjuring up those Dark Age superstitious ideas of madness as the work of the devil.

And all this talk, over and over, of bravery: it would be nice one day if a public figure could talk about having depression without the media using words like 'incredible courage' and 'coming out'. Sure, it is well intentioned. But you shouldn't need to *confess* to having, say, anxiety. You should just be able to tell people. It's an illness. Like asthma or measles or meningitis. It's not a guilty secret. The shame people feel exacerbates symptoms. Yes, absolutely, people are often brave. But the bravery is in living with it, it shouldn't be in *talking about* it. Every time someone tells me I am brave I feel like I should be scared.

Imagine if you were heading for a quiet walk in the forest and someone came up to you.

'Where are you going?' she asks.

'I'm going to the forest,' you tell her.

'Wow,' she gasps, stepping back.

'Wow what?'

And then a tear forms in her eye. She places a hand on your shoulder. 'You're so brave.'

'Am I?'

'So *incredibly* brave. An inspiration, in fact.'

And you would gulp, and go pale, and be permanently put off going into the forest.

Additionally, there is still a lingering toxic idea that people share mental health issues for 'attention'.

That attention people seek can save lives.

But, as C.S. Lewis once put it, 'The frequent attempt to conceal mental pain increases the burden: it is easier to say "My tooth is aching" than to say "My heart is broken".'

We should work towards making this a world where it is easier to talk about our troubles. Talking isn't just about raising awareness. As the various successful types of talk therapy have shown over the last century, talk can have medicinal benefits. It can actually ease symptoms. It heals the teller and the listener through the externalising of internal pain and the knowledge that others feel like we do.

Never stop talking.

Never let other people make you feel it is a weakness or flaw inside you, if you have a mental health problem.

If you have a condition like anxiety, you know that it isn't a weakness. Living with anxiety, turning up and doing stuff with anxiety takes a strength most will never know. We must stop equating the condition with the patient. There needs to be a more nuanced understanding of the different pressures people feel. Walking to a shop can be a show of strength if you are carrying a ton of invisible weight.

Psychogram chart

(pg = psychograms)

Imagine if we could come up with a way to measure psychological weight as we each feel it. Wouldn't that be helpful in bridging the mental and the physical? Wouldn't that help people realise the reality of stress? Wouldn't that help us cope with the stresses of modern life? Humour me. Let's call this imaginary unit a *psychogram*.

'Oh no, I can't check my emails. I've had my limit of psychograms today.'

Walking through a shopping centre	1,298pg
Phone call from the bank	182pg
Job interview	458pg
Watching the news	222pg
A full inbox of unanswered emails	321pg
Your tweet that no one likes	98pg
Guilt from not going to the gym	50pg
Guilt from neglecting to phone close relatives	295pg

Observing how old/overweight/tired you look	177pg
Fear of missing out on a party you see on social media	62pg
Realising you posted a tweet with a spelling mistake	82pg
A worrying symptom you have googled	672pg
Having to do a speech	1,328pg
Looking at images of perfect bodies you'll never have	488pg
Arguing with an online troll	632pg
An awkward date	317pg
Paying utility bills on credit cards	815pg
The realisation that it is Monday and you have to work	701pg
Having your job replaced by a robot	2,156pg
The things you haven't done but wish you had	1,293pg

Note: psychological weight fluctuates greatly. Psychograms are a subjective measurement.

13
THE END OF REALITY

'. . . this collision between one's image of oneself and what one actually is is always very painful and there are two things you can do about it, you can meet the collision head-on and try and become what you really are or you can retreat and try to remain what you thought you were, which is a fantasy, in which you will certainly perish.'

—James Baldwin, *Nobody Knows My Name*

I am what I am what I am

YOU SOMETIMES NEED to go back to move forward. You need to face the pain. The deepest pain. And I've recently felt ready.

I need to go back.

To before the shopping centre.

To a room of surgical whiteness.

'Who am I?' I asked, in the Spanish medical centre, during the beginning phase of my first mental collapse.

Of course, when I am well and calm, the question isn't that scary. Who am I? There is no I. There is no you. Or rather, there are a million Is. A million yous. 'I' is the largest word in the English language.

Behind every you there is another you, and another you and another you, like a Russian doll. Is there a base you? A base me? Or are our identities not Russian dolls but just spirals with no end? Is identity a universe you can never reach the end of but which might lead you back to where you started?

Being relatively well, I enjoy the pointless philosophising

of such questions. Because there is, I suppose, a clear *self* doing the asking. But when I was ill these weren't simply abstract concerns. These were desperate mysteries to solve, as though my life depended on it. Because my life *did* depend on it. The feeling of me-ness had gone – it had been crowded out – and I felt like *I* could become trapped in the *infinite I*, silently floating in panic, with nowhere to land.

Reality versus supermarkets

PANIC ATTACKS OFTEN happen in supermarkets.

I know someone who has had only one panic attack in her life. It happened in a supermarket.

When I used to trawl early noughties message boards for tips on dealing with anxiety, the panic-attack-in-the-supermarket concept came up more than almost any other. I am looking at one thread now that starts: 'WHY DO PANIC ATTACKS STRIKE YOU WHILE SHOPPING IN A SUPERMARKET?'

Panic is there to help us. As it is for many other animals, panic is our mind and body telling us to do something. Fight or flight. Run from the predator or fight the predator. But a supermarket is not a bear or a wolf or a cave-dwelling warrior. You can't fight a supermarket. You can definitely run from one, but that will only increase your chance of having a panic attack the next time you have to go there. It might not just be that supermarket either. If you start playing the avoidance game, it might soon be all supermarkets that become triggers. Then all shops. Then the outside world.

People who have never had a period of living with anxiety and panic don't understand that the *realness* of you is an actual feeling that you can lose. People take it for granted. You don't get up in the morning and think, as you spread peanut butter onto your toast, 'Ah, good, my sense of self is still intact, and the world is still real, I can now get on with my day.' It's just *there*. Until it isn't. Until you are in the cereal aisle, feeling inexplicable terror.

When trying to express what a panic attack feels like it's easy to talk about the obvious symptoms: the racing thoughts, the palpitations, the tightness of the chest, the breathlessness, the nausea, the tingling sensations inside your skull or your arms and legs. But there is another more complicated symptom I used to get. One which I have come to realise is at the heart of what my panic attacks have always been about. It is the one called, tellingly, *derealisation*.

Within a feeling of derealisation, I still *knew* I was me. I just didn't *feel* I was me. It is a feeling of disintegration. Like a sand sculpture crumbling away.

And there is a paradox about this sensation. Because it feels like both an extreme intensity of self and a nothingness of self. A feeling of no return, as if you have suddenly lost something that you didn't know you had to look after, and that the thing you had to look after was you.

And I think the reason supermarkets are such triggers for this is because they are already *derealised*. Supermarkets, like shopping centres, are wholly unnatural places. They might seem old-fashioned now, almost quaint, in this era of online shopping, but they are far more modern than our biology.

The light is not natural light. The humming noise of refrigerators sounds like the ominous soundtrack of an artsy horror movie. The abundance of choice is more than we are naturally built to cope with. The crowds and the shelves are hyperstimulating. And so many of the products themselves aren't natural. I don't just mean because most of them have chemical additives, though that as well. I mean, they have been tampered with. The tins of fish, the bags of salad, the boxes of sweetened puffed rice, the breaded chicken goujons, the processed meat, the vitamin pills, the jars of pre-chopped garlic, the packets of chilli-flavoured sweet potato crisps. They are not natural. And in unnatural settings, when your anxiety is raw enough, you can feel unnatural, too. You can feel as removed from yourself as a packet of toilet roll is removed from a tree. To me, during my panic attacks in supermarkets, the objects on the shelves took on a sinister quality. They seemed alien. And, in a way, they were and *are* alien. They have been taken from where they belong. I related to that. And that is the root of it, I suppose. I didn't feel like *I* belonged. I found it impossible to find a place in such an unnatural and overloaded place. The only thing I knew about myself was the fear. And all the repeated objects in the supermarket were making me worse.

'Objects should not touch because they are not alive,' said Sartre, in *Nausea*, while clearly having a bit of a bad week. 'But they touch me, it is unbearable. I am afraid of being in contact with them as though they were living beasts.'

Objects in a supermarket aren't normal objects either. They are *branded* objects. While products live in a world of physical space, brands seek out mental space. They seek to get into our heads. In many cases companies employ marketing psychologists to do just that. To manipulate us into buying. To toy with our minds.

Caveperson

IMAGINE A CAVEPERSON was frozen for 50,000 years.

Let's call her Su.

Imagine the block of ice she was frozen in suddenly melting in front of your local supermarket.

The caveperson – Su – steps inside. The automatic doors magically close behind her. The light and colours and crowds frighten her. Shopping trolleys appear like strange metallic beasts, domesticated by the humans that push them along. The shining shelves of plastic packaged goods bewilder her. The self-service checkouts are mystifying. The carrier bags look like sacks of strange white skin.

'Unexpected item in bagging area,' the robotic voice says. 'Unexpected item in bagging area . . . Unexpected item in bagging area . . .'

Su begins to panic. She runs towards the window and bangs into the glass.

Su begins to wail. 'Owagh! Agh! Ug-aggh!'

More noises.

The twist at the end of the story arrives.

(Drumroll.)

Su is effectively *Us*.

(Ironic gasp.)

Su is all of us. It's just that we are a bit more used to supermarkets.

We haven't biologically changed for 50,000 years.

But society has, massively. And we are expected to be grateful for all this change. After all, if she hadn't been frozen Su would probably have been killed by a stampede of wild boars at the age of 22 or by a sacrificial ritual at the age of 16. And we *are* lucky. Nothing is luckier than being a living 21st-century human compared to being a Neolithic dead one.

But because of that luck, we need to cherish this life we have. And if we can not only feel *lucky* but also other things – *calm*, *happy*, *healthy* – then why not? Why not know what the world can do to us? Because that knowledge can help us.

It helps me, now, in a supermarket. In shopping centres. In IKEA. On the computer. On a crowded street. In an empty hotel room. Wherever. It helps to know I am just a caveman in a world that has arrived faster than our minds and bodies expected.

Blur

TWO DAYS AGO, I wobbled. I felt the strange psychological pain of grey skies. Picking up my daughter from her dance class, I felt as if I was sinking into the pavement. I began compulsively swallowing, and started to feel the old agoraphobia pitch for an unwanted sequel.

But now I have a little more awareness than I used to have. I could see I hadn't been sleeping well. I'd been working too hard. I'd been worrying too hard about this book. I'd been worried about a million stupid little things. So, I stopped obsessing about emails and stepped away from this Word document and did a moderate 'Yoga for Sleep' video and ate healthily and tried to disconnect. I took the dog for a long walk by the sea.

And I realised: *it doesn't matter. Stop being neurotic.*

Nothing I was worried about would fundamentally change anything. I would still be able to walk the dog. I would still be able to look at the sea. I would still be able to spend time with the people I love.

The anxiety retreated, like a criminal under the spotlight of an investigation.

14
WANTING

'Perhaps when we find ourselves wanting everything it is
because we are dangerously near to wanting nothing.'

—Sylvia Plath

Wishing well

TYPING 'HOW CAN I become' into Google, as I write this, the top five consequent autofill suggestions are:

– rich
– famous
– a model
– a pilot
– an actor

Transcendence

WE ARE BEING sold unhappiness, because unhappiness is where the money is.

Much of what is sold to us is the idea that *we could be better than who we are if we tried to become something else*.

Think about fashion magazines.

Lucinda Chambers served as fashion director of British *Vogue* for 25 years. Shortly after leaving her job, she gave a damning verdict on the industry she had left behind. She declared that, despite their talk of empowerment, few fashion magazines actually make anyone feel empowered. 'Most leave you totally anxiety ridden,' she said in an interview with the fashion journal *Vestoj* that soon went viral, 'for not having the right kind of dinner party, setting the table in the right kind of way or meeting the right kind of people.' In addition, the way fashion magazines focus on unattainably expensive (for most readers) clothes just exacerbates the misery, by making people feel poor.

'In fashion we are always trying to make people buy something they don't need,' said Chambers. 'We don't *need* any more bags, shirts or shoes. So we cajole, bully or encourage people into continuing to buy.'

Fashion magazines and websites and social media accounts sell a kind of transcendence. A way out. A way to escape. But it is often unhealthy, because to make people want to transcend themselves you first have to make them unhappy with themselves.

Yes, people might end up buying a diet book to get the body of a model who endorses it, or a perfume to be more like the image of a celebrity whose name is on the bottle, but that all comes at a cost that is more than financial. People might feel better in the instant hit of the purchase, but in the long term it just feeds a craving to be someone else: someone more glamorous, more attractive, more famous. We are encouraged out of ourselves, to want to have other lives. Lives that are no more real than pots of gold at the end of rainbows.

Maybe the beauty secret no magazine wants to tell us is that the best way to be happy with our looks is to accept the way *we already look*. We are in an age of Photoshop and cosmetic surgery and soon to be in an age of designer robots. It is probably the perfect time to accept our human quirks rather than trying to aim for the blank perfection of an android.

We might think: oh, I need to look a certain way to attract people. Or we could think: actually, there is no better way of filtering out the people who will be no good for me than by looking and being myself.

Being unhappy about your looks is not about your looks: when fashion models develop eating disorders it isn't because they are ugly or overweight. Of course not.

There are various indicators worldwide that eating disorders are on the rise. The non-profit group Eating Disorder Hope reported in 2017 that eating disorders around the world have tended to rise in line with westernisation and industrialisation, and looked at a comprehensive overview of international research. In Asia, for instance, places like Japan, Hong Kong and Singapore have far higher rates than the Philippines, Malaysia and Vietnam, though those latter countries have rapidly rising rates as these countries 'advance' and 'westernise'.

Another telling case is Fiji. Research there has found that eating disorders began to rise in the mid-nineties, just as TV was introduced to the South Pacific island state for the first time. *The New York Times* first reported back in 1999 how eating disorders in Fiji had been virtually unheard of, before TV gave them the slender role models of global hits such as *Melrose Place* and *Beverly Hills 90210*.

Indeed, 'you've gained weight' used to be a common flattering compliment in Fiji, before American television gave girls and young women other body ideals.

In the UK, figures from NHS Digital in 2018 showed that hospital admissions from eating disorders had almost doubled within less than a decade, with girls and twenty-something women most at risk. Caroline Price, from the UK's leading eating disorder charity Beat, told *The Guardian* at the time the figures were published that although eating disorders are 'complex' and down to 'many factors', modern culture has a lot to answer for.

'Eating disorders are on the rise partly because of the challenges of today's society,' she said. 'This includes social media and exam pressure.'

Although these things don't entirely cause the problem, as experts like Price acknowledge, they compound it for those personalities predisposed to eating disorders. According to the UK's National Centre for Eating Disorders (NCED), causal factors include genetics, parents with food issues, fat-teasing, childhood abuse or neglect, childhood trauma, family relationships, having a friend with an eating disorder, and, last but not least, the 'culture'. Particularly problematic is a culture where there is always a new diet to try, and where, according to the NCED website, 'a vulnerable individual internalises the impossibly ideal images they see on TV or in magazines, and continually compares herself unfavourably to those images'.

The website also adds that 'people who can admire a beautiful model but say "I could never look like her but it doesn't bother me too much" are the people who are least likely to fall victim to problems with food'. Maybe there is a lesson for all of us here: in that disconnect between the images we see and the selves we are. We need to build a kind of immune system of the mind, where we can *absorb* but not get *infected by* the world around us.

How to be kinder to yourself about yourself

1. Think of people you have loved. Think of the deepest relationships you have ever had. Think of the joy you felt when seeing those people. Think of how that joy had nothing to do with their looks except that they looked like themselves and you were pleased to see them. Be your own friend. Be pleased to recognise the person behind your face.

2. Change your perspective of how you view photos of yourself. Every photo you look at and think, Oh, I look old, will one day be a photo you look back on and think, Oh, I looked young. Instead of feeling old from the perspective of your younger self, try feeling young from the perspective of your older self.

3. Love imperfections. Accentuate them. They are what will make you different from androids and robots. 'If you look for perfection, you will never be content,' says Lvov's wife, Natalie, in *Anna Karenina*.

4. Don't try to be like someone who already exists. Enjoy your difference.

5. Don't worry when people don't like you. Not everyone will like you. Better to be disliked for being you, than being liked for being someone else. Life isn't a play. Don't rehearse yourself. *Be* yourself.

7. Never let a stranger's negative opinion of you become your own negative opinion of you.

8. If you're feeling bad about yourself, stay away from Instagram.

9. Remember no one else is ever worried about what your face looks like.

10. Do something somewhere in the day that isn't work or duty or the internet. Dance. Kick a ball. Make burritos. Play some music. Play Pac-Man. Stroke a dog. Learn an instrument. Call a friend. Get into a child's pose. Get outside. Go for a walk. Feel the wind on your face. Or lie on the floor and put your feet up against a wall and just breathe.

A note on wanting

IT IS ALL right to want something – fame, the semblance of youth, 10,000 likes, hard abs, doughnuts – but wanting is also lacking. That is what 'want' means. So we have to be careful of our wants and watch that they don't cause too many holes inside us, otherwise happiness will drip through us like water through a leaky bucket. The moment we want is the moment we are dissatisfied. The more we want, the more we will drip ourselves away.

If you were already good enough
what on earth would you
spend your money on?

HAPPINESS IS NOT good for the economy.

We are encouraged, continually, to be a little bit dissatisfied with ourselves.

Our bodies are too fat, or too thin, or too saggy.

Our skin is expected to have the right 'sun-kissed glow', or the right shade of lightness. Depressingly, the global skin lightening industry is a multi-billion-dollar one that is growing year by year.

This is a particularly troubling example, but this central idea of *not feeling good enough* is one that businesses try to exploit almost everywhere. Indeed, it can sometimes seem as though the whole purpose of marketing itself is to make us feel bad about ourselves.

For instance, listen to Robert Rosenthal, author of *Optimarketing: Marketing Optimization to Electrify Your Business*. Back in 2014 he wrote in *Fast Company* magazine that to be successful marketers need to think in terms of the *benefits* of the product, rather than the product's *features*. Sounds innocent, enough, right?

But he adds that benefits often have a 'psychological component'. 'Fear, uncertainty, and doubt, or FUD, is often used legitimately by businesses and organizations to make consumers stop, think, and change their behaviour. FUD is so powerful that it's capable of nuking the competition.'

The success of the campaign is all, for the marketing gurus. The ends justify the means. Let's not think about the wider consequences of making millions of human beings more anxious than they need to be.

But even when an advertising campaign isn't overtly trying to conjure fear, it can still be bad for our psychology. If we are being sold the idea of cool via a pair of trousers, we subconsciously feel a pressure to obtain and maintain that coolness. And all too often, when we have spent a lot of money on a desired item, we have a sinking feeling. The craving for the thing is rarely met by the satisfaction of getting it. And so we crave more. And the cycle repeats. We are encouraged to want what will only make us want more.

We are, in short, encouraged to be addicts.

Never enough

NOTHING IS EVER enough.

I have always been addicted to something. That some-thing changes but the sense of need doesn't.

Drink used to be my thing. I could drink and drink and drink.

When I used to work in an office block, doing a media sales job under the bleak skies of Croydon, I just dreamed of escape. The three pints I drank each night, followed by a vodka Coke, softened the blow of the evening only to harden it again when I woke up the next morning.

Some years after I broke down, I found it suddenly easy to stop drinking. And smoking. And everything. I stopped all stimulants. Even coffee and tea and Coca-Cola. I was in a state of continual panic and pain and would have done anything to take my mind off my mind but by now I knew alcohol wouldn't work. And I thought drugs wouldn't work. I was convinced, by then, that though they clearly worked for other people I was one of the unlucky ones for whom they wouldn't. I was also convinced that I had once had addictive tendencies. It was more difficult to realise I still had them, but that I was now finding 'positive' addictions. Running, for instance, like my dad advised. Yoga. Meditation. Work. Success.

Then, years later, when I felt comparatively better I started drinking again. I wouldn't drink every day, or even every week, but when I did drink I drank irresponsibly. The difference was that this time I could see how alcohol affected my mind. I could see the cycle that happened. I would feel a bit bad – not panic disorder bad, just a general low-level depression – and drink and feel better. Then I would feel hungover and guilty. And this feeling would linger and lower my self-esteem, which would then create more need for distraction. For drink. For eight pints and a gin cocktail. But it was dangerous. It was impossible to be a good husband or father or a good writer when you were that hungover, and the irony was that the feeling of inadequacy and self-loathing made future hangovers more likely. I have learned that however strong the craving gets the guilt afterwards will be stronger. But it's hard. And I have immense sympathy for those who have sought to drown their relentless despair in a sea of booze. And get judged for it in the process by those who have never had that painful yearning to escape themselves.

When people talk about mental health stigma getting better they may be right about an improvement in conditions for people suffering from depression or panic attacks. They probably aren't talking about alcoholism, or self-harm, or psychosis, or Borderline Personality Disorder, or eating disorders, or compulsive behaviours, or drug addiction. Those things can test the open minds of even the best of us. That's the problem with mental illness. It's easy not to judge people for having an *illness*; it's a lot harder not to judge people for how the illness occasionally causes them to *behave*. Because people can't see the reasons.

I can remember going to see the unique, rare genius that was Amy Winehouse in concert and having tears in my eyes at how the crowd – largely drunk themselves – laughed and jeered as she slurred her words between songs and desperately struggled, inebriated, to compose herself. It made me burn with a kind of anger and shame. I tried – ludicrously, embarrassingly – to send silent telepathic messages to her. *It's okay. You'll be okay. They just don't understand.*

Right now, writing this, with the sun outside the window, I am fantasising about a Caipirinha. Brazil's national cocktail. Cachaça, lime, sugar. Heaven in a glass. I have memories of drinking it in shady Spanish squares, and the craving is in part a craving to return back to being carefree and 21 again. But I know that would be a bad idea. I have to remind myself why I want it and what might happen. I have to remember that there wouldn't just be one glass. I have to remember a craving for an innocent drink has previously – after a perfectly respectable afternoon work meeting – ended up with a phone call home from Victoria station at six in the morning after losing my wallet. I have to remember the subsequent spiral into a furious relapse of depression and anxiety – the kind where you end up crying as you stare at your sock drawer and where the sight of grey clouds or a magazine cover prompts feelings of infinite despair. Doing all that remembering, being *mindful* of causes and consequences, makes it a lot easier to resist. An evening of heaven in a glass doesn't outweigh a month of hell in a cage.

My point here isn't specifically about alcohol. It's about how the pattern of addiction – dissatisfaction to temporary solution to increased dissatisfaction – is the model for most of consumer culture. It is also the model for a lot of our relationships with technology. The dangers of excessive technological use are becoming clearer than ever. In 2018,

Apple's CEO, Tim Cook, began to talk about the overuse of technology.

'I don't believe in overuse. I'm not a person that says we've achieved success if you're using it all the time. I don't subscribe to that at all.'

The trouble is, not overusing technology is sometimes easier said than done.

'Make no mistake,' writes neuroscientist Daniel Levitin in his book *The Organized Mind: Thinking Straight in the Age of Information Overload*: 'Email, Facebook, and Twitter checking constitute a neural addiction.' Each time we check social media 'we encounter something novel and feel more connected socially (in a kind of weird impersonal cyber way) and get another dollop of reward hormones' telling us we have 'accomplished something'. But as with all addiction, this feeling of reward is unreliable. As Levitin puts it: 'it is the dumb, novelty-seeking portion of the brain driving the limbic system that induces this feeling of pleasure, not the planning, scheduling, higher-level thought centres in the prefrontal cortex.'

As with living in Ibiza, or in a religious cult, it is hard to see the things we may have problems with if everyone has the same problems. If everyone is spending hour after hour on their phones, scrolling through texts and timelines, then that becomes normal behaviour. If everyone is getting out of bed too early to work 12-hour days in jobs they hate, then why question it? If everyone is worrying about their looks, then worrying about our looks is what we should be doing. If everyone is maxing out their credit cards to pay for things they don't really need, then it can't be a problem. If the whole planet is having a kind of collective break-down, then unhealthy behaviour fits right in. When normality becomes madness, the only way to find sanity is by daring to be different. Or daring to be the you that exists beyond all the physical clutter and mind debris of modern existence.

A paradox

THERE'S A PARADOX about modern hi-tech consumer societies. They seem to encourage *individualism* while not encouraging us – actually forbidding us – to think *as individuals*. They discourage us from standing back from their distractions, like serious addicts have to if they want their life back, and asking: what am I doing? And why do I keep doing it if it doesn't make me happy? In a weird way, this is easier if you choose a socially unacceptable compulsion like heroin addiction than if you have a socially acceptable one like compulsive dieting or tweeting or shopping or working. If the madness is collective and the illness is cultural it can be hard to diagnose, let alone treat.

Even when the tide of society is pulling us in one direction it has to be possible – if that direction makes and keeps us unhappy – to learn how to swim another way. To swim towards the truth of ourselves, a truth our distractions might be hiding. Our very lives might depend on it.

You are more than a consumer

DON'T LET ANYONE or anything make you feel you aren't enough. Don't feel you have to achieve more just to be accepted. Be happy with your own self, minus upgrades. Stop dreaming of imaginary goals and finishing lines. Accept what marketing doesn't want you to: you are fine. You lack nothing.

15

TWO LISTS ABOUT WORK

'How many young college graduates have taken demanding jobs in high-powered firms, vowing that they will work hard to earn money that will enable them to retire and pursue their real interests when they are thirty-five? But by the time they reach that age, they have large mortgages, children to school, houses in the suburbs that necessitate at least two cars per family, and a sense that life is not worth living without really good wine and expensive holidays abroad. What are they supposed to do, go back to digging up roots? No, they double their efforts and keep slaving away.'

—Yuval Noah Harari, *Sapiens: A Brief History of Humankind* (2011)

'I want to say, in all seriousness, that a great deal of harm is being done in the modern world by belief in the virtuousness of work, and that the road to happiness and prosperity lies in an organised diminution of work.'

—Bertrand Russell, *In Praise of Idleness* (1932)

Work is toxic

1. We have become detached from the historic way of working. We, as individuals, rarely consume what we make. People often can't get the work for which they are qualified. Slowly, human work is being taken on by machines. Self-service checkouts. Assembly-line robots. Automated phone operators.

2. Also, the world economy is unfair. Yes, some progress is being made. The numbers of people in extreme povery is falling year by year, according to figures from the World Bank. But other inequalitites are rising. The world's eight richest billionaires own the same wealth as the 3.6 billion people who make up the poorest half of the world, according to a 2017 report from Oxfam. The Western middle classes are shrinking, according to research from Credit Suisse, while the extremes of rich and poor are getting greater. Meritocracy is a hard myth to cling on to.

3. Workplace bullying is rife. The competitive nature of many work environments fuels aggressive rivalry that

can easily tip over into manipulation and bullying. According to research conducted by the University of Phoenix, 75 per cent of workers in America have been affected by workplace bullying, either as a target or a witness. But the targets aren't always who you think. According to the Workplace Bullying Institute, rather than the targets being weaker members of a team, they can often be more skilled and proficient than the bullies – workplace veterans who might be a threat. And research from the TUC in collaboration with the Everyday Sexism Project found that 52 per cent of women said that they had been sexually harassed at work.

4. In extreme cases, workplace stress can be fatal. For instance, between 2008 and 2009 and again in 2014 the French telecoms company Orange reported waves of employee suicides. After the first wave, where 35 employees killed themselves in a matter of months, the boss dismissed it as a 'fashion' although an official report quoted in *The Guardian* blamed a climate of 'management harassment' that had 'psychologically weakened staff and attacked their physical and mental health'.

5. Assessment culture is toxic. The Belgian professor of psychoanalysis, Paul Verhaeghe, believes that the way

work is now set up in our societies, with supervisors supervising supervisors and everyone being watched and marked and continually assessed, is toxic. Even people who aren't in work suffer the same equivalent endless rounds of tests and monitoring. As our school-children are also discovering, all this testing and evaluating makes us stress about the future rather than be comfortable with the present.

6. Work culture can lead to low self-esteem. We are encouraged to believe that success is the result of hard work, that it is down to the individual. So, it is no surprise that when we feel as if we are failing – which is almost continually in an aspirational culture that thrives on raising the bar of our happiness – we take it personally. And think it is down to ourselves. We aren't encouraged to see the context.

7. We like to work. It gives us purpose. But work can also be bad for physical health. In 2015, the Finnish Institute of Occupational Health published a study – the largest ever of its kind – looking at the link between overwork and alcohol. They compiled a dataset of over 333,000 workers across 14 different countries and found, conclusively, that the longer our working hours, the more alcohol we drink.

8. It is hard to challenge our cultural obsession with work. Politicians and business leaders keep up the idea of relentless work as a moral virtue. They talk with misty-eyed sentiment and a dose of sycophancy about 'decent ordinary working people' and 'hard-working families'. We accept the five-day working week as if it was a law of nature. We are often made to feel guilty when we aren't working. We say to ourselves, like Benjamin Franklin did, that 'time is money', forgetting that money is also luck. A lot of people who work very long hours have far less money than people who have never worked in their life.

9. People work ever longer hours, but these extra hours do not guarantee extra productivity. When a Swedish trial experimented with a six-hour working day for nurses in Gothenburg, the results showed that the nurses felt happier and more energised than when they worked for eight hours. They ended up taking fewer sick days, had less physical complaints like back and neck pain, and had an increase of productivity during the hours worked.

10. Our working culture is often dehumanising. We need to assess whether our work is making us ill, or unhappy, and if it is what we can do about it. How

much pressure are we actually putting on ourselves, simply because the way we work makes us feel continually behind? Like life is a race that we are losing? And in our struggle to keep up we don't dare to stop and think what might be good for us.

Ten ways to work without breaking down

1. Try to do something you enjoy. If you enjoy work you will be better at it. If you enjoy work it won't feel like work. Try to think of work as productive play.

2. Aim not *to get more stuff done*. Aim to have *less stuff to do*. Be a work minimalist. Minimalism is about doing more with less. So much of working life seems to be about doing less with more. Activity isn't always the same as achievement.

3. Set boundaries. Have times of the day and week that are work-free, email-free, hassle-free.

4. Don't stress about deadlines. This book is already behind deadline, but you're still reading it.

5. Know that your inbox will never be empty. Accept that.

6. Try to work, where possible, in a way that makes the world a little better. The world shapes us. Making the world better makes us better.

7. Be kind to yourself. If the negatives of the work outweigh the positives of the money, don't do it. If

someone is using their power to bully or harass you, don't stand for it. If you hate your job, and can get away with walking out on your lunch break, walk out on your lunch break. And never go back.

8. Don't think your work matters more than it does. As Bertrand Russell put it: 'One of the symptoms of an approaching nervous breakdown is the belief that one's work is terribly important.'

9. Don't do the work people expect you to do. Do the work you want to do. You only get one life. It's always best to live it as yourself.

10. Don't be a perfectionist. Humans are imperfect. Human work is imperfect. Be less robot, more human. Be more imperfect. Evolution happens through mistakes.

16
SHAPING THE FUTURE

Progress

IT WOULD BE seen as crazily reactionary and conservative to say that technological progress is a uniformly bad thing.

Almost none of us would trade the technology we have now, to live a hundred years ago. Who would give up a world of cars and sat nav and smartphones and laptops and washing machines and Skype and social media and video games and Spotify and X-rays and artificial hearts and cash machines and online shopping? Not me, for sure.

In writing this book I have tried to look at the human psychological cost of the world by looking at the only psychology I truly know – my own. I have written about how we *as individuals* can try to stay sane within a maddening world. The fact that I have had mental illness, though a nightmare in reality, has educated me on the various triggers and torments of the modern world.

The thing I really struggle with, though, is what we can do *as a society*. We can't reverse the clock. We can't suddenly become non-technological, and wouldn't want to. So how do we – the collective we – make a better world for ourselves?

One of the best people to answer this is Yuval Noah Harari, the history professor at the Hebrew University of Jerusalem whose ground-breaking books *Sapiens* and *Homo Deus* question what makes us human, and how technology is not only reshaping our world but also redefining humanity itself. He has written about the nightmarish scenario of a future world where humans could be surpassed by the machines they create and concludes, bleakly, that 'Homo sapiens as we know them will disappear in a century or so'.

After reading Harari's work I wondered why humans are so wilfully ushering in a future that will slowly make themselves redundant. It made me think of another work that had inspired me when I was younger – *Straw Dogs* by the philosopher John Gray – which quite brutally explored the idea that human societal progress is a dangerous myth. After all, we are the only animals that are – as far as we know – obsessed with the idea of progress. If there are turtle historians congratulating previous turtles on their creation of a more enlightened turtle society we don't know about them.

In a piece for *The Observer*, I asked Harari if we should try to resist the idea of the future as one of inevitable technological advancement. Should we try to create a different kind of futurism?

'You can't just *stop* technological progress,' he said. 'Even if one country stops researching artificial intelligence, some other countries will continue to do it. The real question is what to do with the technology. You can use exactly the same technology for very different social and political purposes.'

The internet, of course, would be the obvious case in point in the present. But it is also an example – in the case of what used to be known as the 'world wide web' – of things which started with utopian ideals soon becoming dystopian.

'If you look at the 20th century,' Yuval continued, 'we see that with the same technology of electricity and trains you could create a communist dictatorship or a liberal democracy. And it's the same with artificial intelligence and bioengineering. So, I think people shouldn't be focused on the question of how to stop technological progress because this is impossible. Instead the question should be what kind of usage to make of the new technology. And here we still have quite a lot of power to influence the direction it's taking.'

So, like many things, the answer to fixing the problem seems first to be *aware* of the problem. In other words: the answer to making our minds and our planet healthier and happier is essentially the same one. When Harari said that you can use the same technology for very different purposes, that is of course as true on the micro level of the individual as it is on the macro level of society. Being mindful of how our own use of technology affects us is indirectly being mindful of how technology affects the planet. The planet doesn't simply shape us. We shape the planet by how we choose to live our lives.

And sometimes, when we – and our societies – are heading in unhealthy directions we have to do the bravest and most difficult thing of all. We have to *change*.

That change can take different forms. It can mean using technology to help our minds, by getting an app that limits our social media use, or getting a dimmer switch, or walking more, or being more considerate to people online, or choosing a car less likely to contaminate the air. Being kind to ourselves and being kind to the planet is, ultimately, the *same thing*.

'Progress,' wrote C.S. Lewis, 'means getting nearer to the place you want to be. And if you have taken a wrong turning, then to go forward does not get you any nearer.'

This is a phenomenally good way of looking at it, I think. Forward momentum, on an individual or social level, is not automatically good simply because it is forward momentum. Sometimes we push our lives in the wrong direction. Sometimes societies push themselves in the wrong direction. If we feel it is making ourselves unhappy, progress might mean doing an about-turn and walking back to the right road. But we must never feel – personally or as a culture – that only one version of the future is inevitable.

The future is ours to shape.

Space

IN TERMS OF shaping our own future, spaces are key. We need to make sure there are spaces to be free. To be ourselves. Literal spaces, psychological spaces.

Increasingly, our towns and cities are places which want us there primarily as consumers, rather than people. Which makes it all the more important that we value those threatened spaces where economically irrelevant *being* is still allowed. Forests, parks, state-funded museums and galleries, libraries.

Libraries, for instance, are wonderful places currently at risk. Many people in power dismiss them as irrelevant in the age of the internet. This really misses the point. Many libraries are using the internet in innovative ways, enabling access to books and the internet itself. And besides, libraries aren't just about books. They are one of the few public spaces we have left which don't like our wallets more than us.

But there are other spaces which are threatened, too.

Non-physical spaces. Spaces of time. Digital spaces. Some online companies increasingly want to infringe on our selfhood, seeing us as less of a human being and more as an organism full of data to be mined, or sold on.

There are spaces in the day and week that are being continually devoured in the name of work or other responsibilities.

There are even spaces of the mind that are under threat. The space to think freely, or at least calmly, seems to be harder to find. Which might explain the rise not only in anxiety disorders but also of counterbalancing habits such as yoga and meditation.

People are craving not just physical space but the space to be mentally free. A space from unwanted distracted thoughts that clutter our heads like pop-up advertising of the mind in an already frantic world. And that space is still there to be found. It's just that we can't *rely* on it. We have to consciously seek it out. We might have to set time to read or do some yoga or have a long bath or cook a favourite meal or go for a walk. We might have to switch our phone off. We might have to close the laptop. We might have to unplug ourselves, to find a kind of stripped-back acoustic version of us.

Fiction is freedom

BOOKS MIGHT BE one way to recover some space. Stories. Fiction.

When I was eleven, friendless, struggling to fit in at school, I read *The Outsiders* and *Rumble Fish* and *Tex* by S.E. Hinton, and I suddenly had friends again. Her books were friends. The characters were friends. And real ones, too, because they helped me out. Just as at other times Winnie-the-Pooh and Scout Finch and Pip and *Bonjour Tristesse*'s Cécile were friends. And the stories they inhabited could be places I could hide inside. And feel safe.

In a world that can get too much, a world where we are running out of mind space, fictional worlds are essential. They can be an escape from reality, yes, but not an escape from truth. Quite the opposite. In the 'real' world, I used to struggle with fitting in. The codes you had to follow. The lies you had to tell. The laughs you had to fake. Fiction felt not like an escape from truth but a release into it. Even if it was a truth with monsters or talking bears, there was always some kind of truth there. A truth that could keep you sane, or at least keep you *you*.

For me, reading was never an antisocial activity. It was deeply social. It was the most profound kind of socialising there was. A deep connection to the imagination of another human being. A way to connect without the many filters society normally demands.

So often, reading is seen as important because of its social value. It is tied to education and the economy and so on. But that misses the whole point of reading.

Reading isn't important because it helps to get you a job. It's important because it gives you room to exist beyond the reality you're given. It is how humans merge. How minds connect. Dreams. Empathy. Understanding. Escape.

Reading is love in action.

It doesn't need to be books. But we do need to find that space.

We are frequently encouraged to want the most extreme and exciting experiences. To act on a heady impulse for action. To 'Just Do It' as Nike always used to bark at us, like a self-help drill instructor. As if the very point of life is found via winning a gold medal or climbing Mount Everest or headlining Glastonbury or having a full-body orgasm while sky-diving over the Niagara Falls. And I used to feel the same. I used to want to lose myself in the most intense experiences, as if life was simply a tequila to be slammed. But most of life can't be lived like this. To have a chance of lasting happiness, you have to calm down. You have to just be it as well as just do it.

We crowd our lives with activity because in the West we often feel happiness and satisfaction are achieved by acquisition, by 'seizing' the day, or by going out and 'grabbing' life by the horns. We might sometimes do better to replace life as something to be grabbed at, or reached for, with something we already have. If we clear out the mental clutter we can surely enjoy it more.

The Buddhist monk Thích Nhất Hạnh writes in *The Art of Power* that while 'many people think excitement is happiness', actually 'when you are excited you are not peaceful. True happiness is based on peace.'

Personally, I wouldn't want a life of total neutral inner peace. I'd want to occasionally experience some wild intensity and exhilaration. That is part of me. But I crave that peace and acceptance more than ever.

To be comfortable with yourself, to know yourself, requires creating some inner space where you can *find* yourself, away from a world that often encourages you to lose yourself.

We need to carve out a place in time for ourselves, whether it is via books or meditation or appreciating the view out of a window. A place where we are not craving, or yearning, or working, or worrying, or over-thinking. A place where we might not even be hoping. A place where we are set to neutral. Where we can just breathe, just be, just bathe in the simple animal contentment of being, and not crave anything except what we already have: life itself.

Aim

TO FEEL EVERY moment, to ignore tomorrow, to unlearn all the worries and regrets and fear caused by the concept of time. To be able to walk around and think of nothing but the walking. To lie in bed, not asleep, and not worry about sleep. But just be there, in sweet horizontal happiness, unflustered by past and future concerns.

17

THE SONG OF YOU

Sycamore trees

DURING THE WRITING of this book, my mum had to have a major operation. She had open heart surgery to remove and replace a damaged aortic valve. The operation went well, and she recovered, but her week in intensive care was a bit of a rollercoaster, with doctors and nurses needing to keep a close eye on the levels of oxygen in her blood. They reached worrying lows.

Andrea and I went up and stayed in a hotel near the hospital. I sat by her bedside with my dad as Mum slid in and out of sleep. I helped spoon-feed her hospital meals and brought in carrier bags full of shop-bought smoothies, and the occasional newspaper for Dad. My worry about Mum stripped everything else away. I felt incredible guilt about having hardly listened when she had told me about her initial visits to the doctor.

Now, I didn't care about any urgent emails I hadn't got back to. I didn't have any temptation to check social media. Even world news seemed like a background irrelevance when you were sitting in an intensive care unit hearing the wails of grief coming from beyond a thin hospital curtain as the patient in the next bed passes away.

Intensive care units are bleak places, sometimes, but those sterile rooms full of people perched between life and death can also be hopeful ones. And the nurses and doctors were an inspiration.

It's just a shame, I suppose, that it takes such major events in our lives, or in the lives of the people we love, for perspective to arrive. Imagine if we could keep hold of that perspective. If we could *always* have our priorities right, even during the good and healthy times. Imagine if we could always think of our loved ones the way we think of them when they are in a critical condition. If we could always keep that love – love that is always there – so close to the surface. Imagine if we could keep the kindness and soft gratitude towards life itself.

I am trying now, when my life gets too packed with unnecessary stressful junk, to remember that room in the hospital. Where patients were thankful just to look at the view out of a window. Some sunshine and sycamore trees.

And where life, on its own, was everything.

Love

Only love will save us.

Minus psychograms
(things that make you feel lighter)

Imagine that, as well as psychograms, there could be things that make your mind feel lighter. We could call these minus psychograms, or -pg.

The sun appearing unexpectedly from behind a cloud	57-pg
The all-clear from a doctor	320-pg
Being on holiday somewhere with no wi-fi (after the initial panic)	638-pg
Walking the dog	125-pg
A yoga session	487-pg
Being lost in a good book	732-pg
Arriving home after a terrible train journey	398-pg
Being surrounded by nature	1,291-pg
Dancing	1,350-pg
A close relative recovering from an operation	3,982-pg

And so on.

Sri Lanka

I HAD BEEN asked to visit the beautiful fort city of Galle, on the southwest coast of Sri Lanka, to attend the literature festival there and give a talk on mental health. The event was quite special, as Sri Lanka is still a place where talking about mental illness can be taboo. And it was emotional, hearing stories of anxiety and depression and OCD and suicidal tendencies and bipolar disorder and schizophrenia in a context where they aren't normally publicly aired. It was like you could *feel* stigma evaporating in real time.

But it wasn't the event I remember, it was the day after. On Hikkiduwa beach, alongside locals and backpackers, feeding giant sea turtles seaweed straight from my hand. Andrea and the children were there. It was the kind of moment I never believed I would have when I was an agoraphobic twentysomething convinced I wouldn't live to reach 30, having pushed everyone I loved away. Then, at 40, in the Southern Hemisphere, there I was with people I loved, on an idyllic beach, close up to these large ancient reptiles. They seemed so calm and wise in their longevity. I wondered what secret wisdom they had. And wished there was a way for a human to ask a turtle questions.

So, when depression slugs over me I close my eyes and enter the bank of good days and think of sunshine and laughter and turtles. And I try to remember how possible the impossible can sometimes be.

An amphibious approach to life

'Hello, turtle.'

'Oh. Hi there.'

'Any advice on life?'

'Why are you asking me?'

'Because you're a turtle.'

'And?'

'Turtles have survived for millions of years. You've been around for 157 million years. That's more than 700 hundred times as long as Homo sapiens have been around. You must know some things, as a species.'

'You're conflating length of existence with breadth of knowledge.'

'It's just humans who have made a mess of the world. Turtles don't seem to.'

'I know. We are near extinction because of you.'

'I'm sorry.'

'I was using "you" in the plural sense. But also, yes, you.'

'I know. I'm a human. I share the blame.'

'Yes. You do.'

'Yes.'

'Anyway, if you really want to know, the advice I would give is stop it.'

'Stop *what*?'

'It. The rushing after nothing. Humans seem in such a rush to escape where they are. Why? Is it the air? Does it not hold you up well enough? Maybe you need more time in the sea. I would say: stop it. Don't just take your time, *be your time*. Move fast or slow, but be aware you will always take yourself with you. Be happy to paddle in the water of existence.'

'Right.'

'Look at my head. It's tiny. My brain-to-body-mass ratio is embarrassing. But it doesn't matter, you see. If you take life carefully, you can focus. You can be how you need to be. You can have an amphibious approach to life. You can be at one with the rhythms of the whole earth. The wet and the dry. You can tune in to the wind and the water. You can tune in to yourself. It's rather wonderful, you know, being a turtle.'

'I bet. Thanks, turtle.'

'Now, may I have some more seaweed?'

Reversing the loop

ANXIETY IS SELF-PERPETUATING. When you have it in its illness form it is a feedback loop of despair. The only way out is to stop the meta-worry, to stop worrying *about* the worrying, which is near impossible. Sometimes the trick is to find a reverse kind of loop. I do this by accepting that I am in this state of non-acceptance. By being comfortable with being uncomfortable. By accepting I don't have control.

A cliché but true: you can't get to where you want to be without first accepting where you are. The world tries to tell us not to accept ourselves. It makes us want to be richer, prettier, thinner, happier. To want more. When we are ill, this becomes doubly true, and yet this is when we most need to accept ourselves, accept the moment of pain, in order to release it. Slowly release it, into the world from which it came.

The sky is always the sky

JUST NOW I looked out of the window and felt calmer. The moon is a real flirt tonight behind a veil of bruise-blue cloud. This sky is sensational. No photo would catch it.

And this reminded me of something. When I had a long episode of depression about a decade ago, the worst depression I have had since my breakdown in my twenties, one of the few comforts I used to get was looking at the sky. We lived in Yorkshire, and there wasn't that much light pollution, and so the sky was vast and clear. I'd take the bins out and just look at the night sky and feel myself and my pain getting smaller. I'd stand there for a while breathing the cool air, staring at stars and planets and constellations. I would breathe deeply, as if the cosmos was something you could inhale. I'd sometimes place my hand on my stomach and feel the stuttery flutter of my nervous breathing begin to settle.

I often wondered, and still wonder, why the sky, especially the night sky, had such an effect. I used to think it was to do with the scale. When you look up at the cosmos you can't help but feel minuscule. You feel the smallness of yourself not only in space but also in time. Because, of course, when you stare into space you are staring up at ancient history. You are staring at stars as they *were*, not as they *are*. Light travels. It doesn't just instantaneously appear. It moves at 186,000 miles per second. Which sounds fast, but also means that light from the closest star to Earth (after the sun) took over four years to get here.

But some of the stars visible to the naked eye are over 15,000 light years away. Which means the light reaching your eye began its journey at the end of the Ice Age. Before humans knew how to farm land. Contrary to popular belief, most of the stars that we see with our eyes are not dead. Stars, unlike us, exist for a very long time. But that adds to, rather than takes away from, the therapeutic majesty of the night sky. Our beautiful but tiny brief role within the cosmos is as that rarest of galactic things: a living, breathing, conscious organism.

When looking at the sky, all our 21st-century worries can be placed in their cosmic context. The sky is bigger than emails and deadlines and mortgages and internet trolls. It is bigger than our minds, and their illnesses. It is bigger than names and nations and dates and clocks. All of our earthly concerns are quite transient when compared to the sky. Through our lives, throughout every chapter of human history, the sky has always been the sky.

And, of course, when we are looking at the sky we aren't looking at something outside ourselves. We are looking, really, at where we came from. As physicist Carl Sagan wrote in his masterpiece *Cosmos*: 'The nitrogen in our DNA, the calcium in our teeth, the iron in our blood, the carbon in our apple pies were made in the interiors of collapsing stars. We are made of starstuff.'

The sky, like the sea, can anchor us. It says: hey, it's okay, there is something bigger than your life that you are part of, and it's – literally – cosmic. It's the most wonderful thing. And you need to make like a tree or a bird and just feel a part of the great natural order now and again. You are incredible. You are nothing and everything. You are a single moment and all eternity. You are the universe in motion.

Well done.

Nature

THE SKY HAS been shown to soothe us.

In 2018 a research study conducted by King's College London found that being able to see the sky helps our mental health. And not just the sky. Seeing trees, hearing birdsong, being outside, and feeling in contact with nature.

Participants in the study went out into the world, and were instructed to record their mental states at different locations. Interestingly, the study was quite nuanced as it factored in each individual's risk of developing poor mental health by doing some early tests on each participant to assess impulsive behaviours.

The study, catchily titled 'Urban Mind: Using Smartphone Technologies to Investigate the Impact of Nature on Mental Wellbeing in Real Time', found that while being out in the natural world is good for everyone, it is of particular benefit for those who are more predisposed to mental health problems like addiction, ADHD, antisocial personality disorder and bipolar disorder.

'Short-term exposure to nature has a measurable beneficial impact on mental wellbeing,' concluded Dr Andrea Mechelli, who had helped to lead the research.

Ecotherapy or 'green care' projects are on the rise. Many city farms and community gardens are now used for mental health work to lower stress, anxiety and depression. Of course, in many ways this is all acting on old advice: 'Get yourself some fresh air.' In 1859, in her *Notes on Nursing*, Florence Nightingale wrote that 'after a closed room, what hurts them [patients] most is a dark room' and advised that 'it is not only light but direct sunlight they want'. Finally, evidence is catching up.

The trouble is, over half the world's population now live in big cities. In 1950 more than two-thirds of the world's population lived in rural settlements. Now, worldwide, most people live in urban areas. And, as people spend more time indoors than ever before, it's clear that we aren't existing much amid forests and under natural skies.

It's time we started being more aware that the blues and greens of nature can help us. And the lives of children, too. More fresh air, more direct sunlight, maybe even if we are lucky the odd walk across fields and through forests. And perhaps also, armed with evidence, we can help to make the communal urban spaces we inhabit a bit more green and pleasant, too, so that everyone can benefit from nature, not just the lucky few.

The world inside

SO, YES, THE beauty of nature can heal. But in Ibiza, in 1999, I stood on top of a cliff near the villa where I was living, tucked into one of the quieter corners on the east of the island, and urged myself to jump.

I literally had no way of coping – or none that I could see – with the mental pain and confusion I was going through, and wished I had no one who cared about me, so I could just leave and disappear with minimal impact.

I sometimes think of that cliff edge. Of the scrubby grass I stood on, of the glittering sea I stared out at, and the limestone coastline stretching out. None of that, at the time, consoled me. Nature is shown to be good for us, but in the moment of crisis nothing helps. No view in the world could have made me feel any better in that moment of extreme invisible pain. That view won't have changed much over two decades. And yet I could stand there now and feel its beauty, and feel so different to the terrified young man I had been.

The world affects us, but it isn't quite *us*. There is a space inside us that is independent to what we see and where we are. This means we can feel pain amid external beauty and peace. But the flipside is that we can feel calm in a world of fear. We can cultivate a calmness inside us, one that lives and grows, and gets us through.

There is a cliché about reading. That there are as many books as there are readers. Meaning every reader has their own take on a book. Five people could sit down and read, say, *The Left Hand of Darkness* by Ursula K. Le Guin and have five totally different legitimate responses. It isn't really about what you read, but how you read it. The writer might start a story but they need a reader for it to come alive, and it never comes alive the same way twice. The story is never just the words. It is also the reading of them. And that is the variable. That is where the magic lives. All a writer can do is provide a match, and hopefully a dry one. The reader has to strike the flame into being.

The world is like that, too. There are as many worlds as there are inhabitants. The world exists in you. Your experience of the world isn't this objective unchangeable thing called 'The World'. No. Your experience of the world is your interaction with it, your interpretation of it. To a certain degree we all make our own worlds. We read it in our own way. But also: we can, to a degree, choose what to read. We have to work out what about the world makes us feel sad or scared or confused or ill or calm or happy.

We have to find, within all those billions of human worlds, the one we want to live on. The one that, without us imagining it, would never arrive.

And, likewise, we have to understand that however it might influence them, the world is not our feelings. We can feel calm in a hospital, or in pain on a Spanish clifftop.

We can contradict ourselves. We can contradict the world. We can sometimes even do the impossible. We can live when death seems inevitable. And we can hope after we knew hope had gone.

You, unplugged

LIFE CAN SOMETIMES feel like an overproduced song, with a cacophony of a hundred instruments playing all at once. Sometimes the song sounds better stripped back to just a guitar and a voice. Sometimes, when a song has too much happening, it's hard to hear the song at all.

And like that overcrowded song we, too, can feel a bit lost.

Our natural selves haven't changed in tens of thousands of years, and we should remember that, with every new app or smartphone or social media platform or nuclear weapon we design. We should remember the song of being human. To think of the air when we feel stuck under-water. To find some calm amid an age of saturated marketing and breaking news and the million daily jolts of the internet. To be unafraid of being afraid. To be our own brilliant, true, beautiful, fragile, flawed, imperfect, animal, ageing, wonderful selves, trapped in time and space, made free by our ability to stop, at any moment, and find some-thing – a song, a sunbeam, a conversation, a piece of pretty graffiti – and feel the sheer improbable wonder of being alive.

18

EVERYTHING
YOU ARE IS ENOUGH

'There is only one corner of the universe you can be certain of improving, and that's your own self.'

—Aldous Huxley

Things that have almost always been

CLIFFS. TREE FERNS. Companionship. Sky. The man in the moon. The sentimentality of sunrises and sunsets. Eternal love. Dizzy lust. Abandoned plans. Regret. Cloudless night skies. Full moons. Morning kisses. Fresh fruit. Oceans. Seas. Tides. Rivers. Lakes as still as mirrors. Faces full of friendship. Comedy. Laughter. Stories. Myths. Songs. Hunger. Pleasure. Sex. Death. Faith. Fire. The deep silent goodness of the observing self. The light made brighter by the dark around it. Eye contact. Dancing. Meaningless conversation. Meaningful silence. Sleep. Dreams. Nightmares. Monsters made of shadows. Turtles. Sawfish. The fresh green of wet grass. The bruised purple of clouds at dusk. The wet crash of waves on slow-eroding rocks. The dark slick shine of wet sand. The gasping relief of a thirst quenched. The terrible, tantalising awareness of being alive. The now that for ever is made of. The possibility of hope. The promise of home.

What I tell myself when things get too much

1. It's okay.
2. Even if it isn't okay, if it's a thing you can't control, don't try to control it.
3. You feel misunderstood. Everyone is misunderstood. Don't worry about other people understanding you. Aim to understand yourself. Nothing else will matter after that.
4. Accept yourself. If you can't be happy as yourself, at least accept yourself as you are right now. You can't change yourself if you don't know yourself.
5. Never be cool. Never try to be cool. Never worry what the cool people think. Head for the warm people. Life is warmth. You'll be cool when you're dead.
6. Find a good book. And sit down and read it. There will be times in your life when you'll feel lost and confused. The way back to yourself is through reading. I want you to remember that. The more you read,

the more you will know how to find your way through those difficult times.

7. Don't fix yourself down. Don't be blinded by the connotations of your name, gender, nationality, sexuality or Facebook profile. Be more than data to be harvested. 'When I let go of what I am,' said the Chinese philosopher Lao Tzu, 'I become what I might be.'

8. Slow down. Also Lao Tzu: 'Nature does not hurry, yet everything is accomplished.'

9. Enjoy the internet. Don't use it when you aren't enjoying it. (Nothing has sounded so easy and been so hard.)

10. Remember that many people feel like you. You can even go online and find them. This is one of the most therapeutic aspects of the social media age. You can find an echo of your pain. You can find someone who will understand.

11. As Yoda nearly put it, you can't *try* to be. Trying is the opposite of being.

12. The things that make you unique are flaws. Imperfections. Embrace them. Don't seek to filter out your human nature.

13. Don't let marketing convince you that happiness is a

commercial transaction. As the Cherokee-American cowboy Will Rogers once put it, 'Too many people spend money they haven't earned, to buy things they don't want, to impress people they don't like.'

14. Never miss breakfast.

15. Go to bed before midnight most days.

16. Even during manic times – Christmas, family occasions, hectic work patches, city holidays – find some moments of peace. Retreat to a bedroom now and then. Add a comma to your day.

17. Shop less.

18. Do some yoga. It's harder to be stressed out if your body and your breath isn't.

19. When times get rocky, keep a routine.

20. Do not compare the worst bits of your life with the best bits of other people's.

21. Value the things most that you'd miss the most if they weren't there.

22. Don't try to pin yourself down. Don't try to understand, once and for all, who you are. As the philosopher Alan Watts said, 'trying to define yourself is like trying to bite your own teeth'.

23. Go for a walk. Go for a run. Dance. Eat peanut butter on toast.

24. Don't try to feel something you don't feel. Don't try to be something you can't be. That energy will exhaust you.

25. Connecting with the world has nothing to do with wi-fi.

26. There is no future. Planning for the future is just planning for another present in which you will be planning for the future.

27. Breathe.

28. Love now. Love right now. If you have someone or something to love, do it this instant. Love fearlessly. As Dave Eggers wrote: 'It is no way to live, to wait to love.' Throw love out there selflessly.

29. Don't feel guilty. It is almost impossible, unless you are a sociopath, not to feel some guilt these days. We are cluttered with guilt. There is the guilt we learned at childhood mealtimes, the guilt of eating while knowing there are starving people in the world. The guilt of privilege. The eco-guilt of driving a car or flying in a plane or using plastic. The guilt of buying stuff that may be unethical in some way we can't quite see. The guilt of unspoken or unfaithful desires. The guilt of not being the things other people wanted you to be. The guilt of taking up space. The guilt of not

being able to do things other people can do. The guilt of being ill. The guilt of living. It's useless, this guilt. It doesn't help anyone. Try to do good right now, without drowning in whatever bad you might once have done.

30. See yourself outside market forces. Don't compete in the game. Resist the guilt of non-doing. Find the uncommodified space inside us. The true space. The human space. The space that could never be measured in terms of numbers or money or productivity. The space that the market economy can't see.

31. Look at the sky. (It's amazing. It's always amazing.)

32. Spend some time with a non-human animal.

33. Be unashamedly boring. Boring can be healthy. When life gets tough, aim for those beige emotions.

34. Don't value yourself in line with other people's valuation of yourself. As Eleanor Roosevelt said, 'No one can make you feel inferior without your consent.'

35. The world can be sad. But remember a million unsung acts of kindness happened today. A million acts of love. Quiet human goodness lives on.

36. Don't beat yourself up for being a mess. It's fine. The universe is a mess. Galaxies are drifting all over the place. You're just in tune with the cosmos.

37. If you're feeling mentally unwell, treat yourself as you would any physical problem. Asthma, flu, whatever. Do what you need to do to get better. And have no shame about it. Don't keep walking around on a broken leg.

38. It's okay to cry. People cry. Women cry. And *men* cry. They have tear ducts and lachrymal glands just like other human beings. A man crying is no different from a woman crying. It's natural. Social roles are toxic when they don't allow an outlet for pain. Or sentimental emotion. Cry, human. Cry your heart out.

39. Allow yourself to fail. Allow yourself to doubt. Allow yourself to feel vulnerable. Allow yourself to change your mind. Allow yourself to be imperfect. Allow yourself to resist dynamism. Allow yourself not to shoot through life like an arrow speeding with purpose.

40. Try to want less. A want is a hole. A want is a lack. That is part of the definition. When the poet Byron wrote 'I want a hero' he meant that he didn't have one. The act of wanting things we don't need makes us feel a lack we didn't have. Everything you need is here. A human being is complete just being human. We are our own destination.

Diminishing returns

PLANET EARTH IS unique. It is the only place we know of where life exists in the vast cosmic arena of the universe. It is an incredible place. On its own, it gives us everything humans need to survive.

And you are also incredible. Equally so. You were incredible from the day you were born. You were *everything* from the day you were born. No one looks at a newborn baby and thinks, oh dear, look at all that *absence of stuff*. They look at a baby and they feel like they are looking at perfection, untainted by the complexities and baggage of life yet to come.

We come complete. Give us some food and drink and shelter, sing us a song, tell us a story, give us people to talk to and care for and fall in love with and there you go. A *life*.

But somewhere along the way we have raised the threshold of what we need, or feel we need, to be happy.

We are encouraged to buy stuff to make ourselves happy because companies are encouraged to make more money to make themselves more successful. It is also addictive. It isn't addictive because it makes us happy. It is addictive because it *doesn't* make us happy. We buy something and we enjoy it – we enjoy the *newness* of it – for a little while but then we get used to having it, we acclimatise, and so we need something else. We need to feel that sense of change, of variety. Something newer, something better, something upgraded. And the same thing happens again.

And over time we get used to more and more stuff.

And this applies to everything.

The Instagrammer who enjoys getting a lot of likes for their selfie will soon seek more likes, and be disappointed if the number stays the same. The grade A student will come to feel like a failure if they get a single B. The entrepreneur who becomes rich will seek to earn more money. The gym-goer who likes their new sculpted body will want to train harder, and harder. The worker who gets the promotion they wanted will soon want another one. With every achievement, acquisition or purchase the bar is raised.

I once thought I'd be happy for ever if I got articles published. Then a book published. Then if I could get *another* book published. Then if a book became a bestseller. And then if another one could. Then if it became a *number one* bestseller. Then if the film rights were sold. And so on. And I did, like lots of people, get happy, fleetingly, at each career goal I set myself, but my mind quickly got used to the previous achievement and found a new goal. So, the more I got, the more I needed to get in order to stay level.

The more 'success' you get, the easier it is to be disappointed by not getting things. The only difference is that now no one feels sorry for you.

No matter what we buy or achieve, the feelings don't last. A sports champion always wants another win. The millionaire always wants another million. The spotlight-hungry star wants more fame. Just as the alcoholic wants another drink and the gambler wants another bet.

But there are always going to be diminishing returns.

The child with a hundred toys is going to play with each new one less and less.

And think about it. If you could afford a holiday ten times more expensive than your last holiday, would you feel ten times more relaxed? I doubt it. If you could spend ten times longer looking at your Twitter feed, would you be ten times more informed? Of course not. If you spent twice as long at work would you get twice as much done?

Research suggests you wouldn't. If you could buy a car ten times more expensive than your current one would it get you from A to B ten times quicker? Nope. If you bought more anti-ageing creams would you age less with each extra purchase? Also nope.

You are conditioned to want more. Often this conditioning comes from companies who themselves are conditioned, collectively, to want more. Wanting more is the default setting.

But just as there is only one planet – a planet with finite resources – there is also only one you. And you also have a finite resource – time. And, let's face it, you can't multiply yourself. An overloaded planet cajoles us into overloaded lives but, ultimately, you can't play with all the toys. You can't use all the apps. You can't be at all the parties. You can't do the work of 20 people. You can't be up to speed on all the news. You can't wear all eleven of your coats at once. You can't watch every must-see show. You can't live in two places at once. You can buy more, you can acquire more, you can work more, you can earn more, you can strive more, you can tweet more, you can watch more, you can want more, but as each new buzz diminishes there comes a point where you have to ask yourself: what is all this for?

How much extra happiness am I acquiring? Why am I wanting so much more than I need?

Wouldn't I be happier learning to appreciate what I already have?

Simple ideas for a new beginning

– *Awareness*. Be aware of how much time you are spending on your phone, of how much the news is messing with your mind, of how your attitudes to work are changing, of how many pressures you feel, and how many of them stem from problems of modern life, of being connected into the world's nervous system. Awareness becomes a solution. Just as being aware of your hand on a hot stove means you can take your hand off the stove, being aware of the invisible sharks of modern life helps you to avoid them.

– *Wholeness*. The deficiencies you are made to feel, that society seems to *want* you to feel, you don't have to feel. You were born how you were meant to be, and remain so. You will never be anyone else, so don't try to be. You have no understudy. You are the one who is here to be you. So, don't compare, don't judge yourself on the opinion of people who have never been you.

– *The world is real, but* your *world is subjective*. Changing your perspective changes your planet. It can change your life. One version of multiverse theory states that we create a new universe with every decision we make. You can sometimes enter a better universe simply by not checking your phone for ten minutes.

– *Less is more*. An overloaded planet leads to an overloaded mind. It leads to late nights and light sleep. It leads to worrying about unanswered emails at three in the morning. In extreme cases, it leads to panic attacks in the cereal aisle. It's not 'Mo Money Mo Problems', as the Notorious B.I.G. track once put it. It's more everything, more problems. Simplify your life. Take away what doesn't need to be there.

– *You already know what is significant*. The things that matter are obviously the things you would truly miss deeply if they were gone. These are the things you should spend your time on, when you can. People, places, books, food, experiences, whatever. And sometimes to enjoy these more you have to strip other things back. You need to break free.

The important stuff

A WEEK AGO I went to a charity shop with stuff I'd accumulated and offloaded it. It felt good. Not only charitable, but cleansing. The house is free of a lot of my clutter now. Clothes I never wear, aftershaves I've never sprayed, two chairs no one sits on, old DVDs I'll never watch again, even – gasp – some books I will never read.

'Are you sure you want to get rid of all this?' Andrea had asked, staring at the landscape of bin bags in the hallway. Even she – a natural-born clearer-outer – was taken aback.

'Yeah. Think so.'

The thing is that in the actual process of throwing things out, I ended up valuing the things I had more. For instance, while I was discarding some old DVDs I discovered one I not only wanted to keep, but also re-watch. *It's a Wonderful Life*. And I watched it two nights later.

I definitely don't want to give you a fear of missing out – and it's hardly *of the moment* – but if you have never watched *It's a Wonderful Life* try to. It's not schmaltzy. It's earnest and sentimental, yes, but honestly so. It's raw. It has incredible power. About the big importance of small lives. About why we matter. About the difference a life can make. About why we should stay alive. That film is never a waste of time. It helps you value time.

This is just an example of how removing the mediocre stuff that clogs up your time and living room helps to highlight the good stuff. Similarly, limiting your access to news helps you to prioritise what's important when you do catch up with it. Working fewer hours helps to make those hours more productive. And so on. Declutter. Edit your life.

But, to be honest, the clearing out was actually the easy bit. It's easy to halve the number of clothes in your wardrobe. It's easy to put a better filter on your emails and to turn off your notifications. It's easy to be kinder to people online. It's *relatively* easy to go to bed a bit earlier. It's *relatively* easy to become more aware of your breathing, and to make time for half an hour of yoga a day. It's *relatively* easy to charge your phone overnight *outside* your bedroom. (Okay, that's still a hard one, but I'm doing it.)

The really difficult bit is how to change attitudes inside yourself. How do you edit those?

Those attitudes ingrained in you by society. Attitudes about what you need to do and be to be valued. Attitudes about how you should be working or earning or consuming or watching or living. Attitudes about how your mental health is separate from your physical health. Attitudes about all the things you are encouraged by marketers and politicians to fear. About all the wants and lacks you are supposed to feel in order to keep the economy and social order going.

Yes. Not easy. But acceptance seems to be the key.

Accepting who you are. Accepting the reality of society, but also the reality of yourself, and not feeling like you're incomplete. It's that feeling of lacking that fills our houses and minds with clutter. Try to stay your full self. A complete, whole human being, here for no other purpose than to be you.

'The thing is to free one's self,' wrote Virginia Woolf, struggling with the task. 'To let it find its dimensions, not be impeded.'

By the way, I would be lying if I said I was there already. I am so not there. I am closer, but not even vaguely there. I doubt I will ever be totally there, in that blissful state of nirvana beyond the nervous world of technology and consumerism and distraction. With a mind as clear as a mountain stream. There is no finishing line. It's not about being perfect. In fact, punishing yourself for not being perfect is part of the whole problem. So, accepting where I am – improved and imperfect – is an ongoing task, but a massively rewarding one.

Knowing the things that are unhealthy makes it a lot easier to protect yourself.

It's the same with food and drink. If you know chocolate bars and Coca-Cola are unhealthy then it doesn't mean you are never going to consume them. But it possibly means you might have less of them, and maybe even enjoy them more when you have them, as it becomes more special.

So, instead of block-watching five hours of TV I now just try to watch a single show.

Instead of spending a whole afternoon on social media, I'll spend the occasional ten minutes, always noting the time on the computer when I log on so I can keep track. I try to do kind deeds and good things where I can. Nothing heroic, but the usual – give a bit to charity, talk with the homeless, help people with their mental health, offer up a train seat. Little micro-kindnesses. Not just to be selfless but because doing good things is quite healing. It makes you feel good. A type of psychological decluttering. Because kindness spring-cleans the soul. And maybe makes this nervous planet a little less nervous.

It is an ongoing thing. I try to be okay with myself. To not feel like I have to work or spend or exercise my way into accepting myself. That I don't need to be tough and invulnerable to be a man. That I don't have to worry about what other people think of me. And even when I feel weak, even when I get all those unwanted thoughts and fears, all that *mind spam*, I try to stay calm. I try not to even try. I try just to accept the way I am. I accept what I feel. And then I can understand it, and change the way I interact with the world.

The world is inside you

YOU MAY BE a part of the planet. But, equally, the planet is part of you. And you can choose how you respond to it. You can change the parts that get in. Yes, in one sense, it is easy to see that the planet is exhibiting symptoms similar to an individual with an anxiety disorder, but there is no *one* version of the world. There are seven billion versions of the world. The aim is to find the one that suits you best.

And remember.

Everything special about humans – our capacity for love and art and friendship and stories and all the rest – is not a product of modern life, it is a product of *being a human*. And so, while we can't disentangle ourselves from the transient and frantic stress of modern life, we can place an ear next to our human self (or soul, if you'd rather) and listen to the quiet stillness of being. And realise that we don't need to distract ourselves from ourselves.

Everything we need is right here. Everything we are is enough. We don't need the bigger boat to deal with the invisible sharks around us. We *are* the bigger boat. The brain, as Emily Dickinson put it, is bigger than the sky. And by noticing how modern life makes us feel, by allowing that reality and by being broad-minded enough to change when change is healthy, we can engage with this beautiful world without being worried it will steal who we are.

Beginning

I LOOK AT the clock on my computer.

I do this now to keep track of how long I spend staring at a screen. Simply knowing the amount makes you spend less time at a computer. I suppose that's the key: being aware.

Another awareness. I am aware of the dog, now, beside my feet.

And I am also aware of the view.

The sun is shining outside my window. I can see the sea in the distance. An offshore wind farm on the horizon, little lines of hope. A criss-cross of telegraph wires slicing the scene like lines in an abstract painting. Rooftops and chimneys pointing towards the sky we rarely observe.

I stare at the sea, and it calms me. And I am trying to be in tune with what it is about this world that makes us feel good. This is how we can live in the present. This is how every single moment becomes a beginning. By being aware. By stripping away the stuff we don't need and finding what our self really requires. And from that awareness we can find a way to keep hold of ourselves and still stay in love with this world.

That's the idea. It's hard. It's so bloody hard. But also, it is better than despair. And so long as you make sure it isn't something else you can fail at, once you accept your messy flaws and failures as natural, then it becomes a lot easier.

Later today I will be going to a shopping centre. I don't *enjoy* shopping centres, but I no longer have panic attacks in them. The key to surviving shopping centres and supermarkets and negative online comments or anything else is not to ignore them, or to run from them, or to fight them, but to allow them to be. Accept you don't have any control over them, only over yourself.

'For after all,' wrote the poet Henry Wadsworth Longfellow, 'the best thing one can do when it is raining is let it rain.' Yes. Let it rain. Let the planet be. You have no choice. But also, be aware of your feelings, good and bad. Know what works for you and accept what doesn't. When you know the rain is rain, and not the end of the world, it makes things easier.

But, right now, it isn't raining.

And so, the second after finishing this page, I am going to save this document and close the laptop and head outside.

Into air and sunlight.

Into life.

People I'd like to thank

I WOULD LIKE to thank all the people I have met in real life or online over the last few years who have found the courage to talk about their mental health. The more we talk, the more we encourage others to do the same.

Although books have, ridiculously, only one name on the front they are typically a team effort, and this one more than most. Firstly, I owe infinite and ongoing gratitude to my great, warm, fearless and tireless agent Clare Conville, and everyone who works with her at C+W and Curtis Brown.

I must thank my wonderful and long-suffering editor Francis Bickmore at Canongate, and all the other clever people who read early versions including my brilliant editors across the ocean – my US editor Patrick Nolan at Penguin Random House, and Kate Cassaday at HarperCollins Canada. Also, this book would not be *this* book without the sharp eyes of Alison Rae, Megan Reid, Leila Cruickshank, Jo Dingley, Lorraine McCann, Jenny Fry and Canongate head honcho Jamie Byng. Thanks also to Pete Adlington for his sumptuous work on the cover and all the team at Canongate who have worked so hard on this book and my others, including Andrea Joyce, Caroline Clarke, Jess Neale, Neal Price, Alice Shortland, Lucy Zhou and Vicki Watson.

Thanks to all the social media friends who have allowed me to quote them in this book.

Of course, thanks to Andrea, for being this book's first and most honest reader and for being someone who makes life on this nervous planet less nerve-racking. And apologies to Pearl and Lucas for this book ironically causing me to spend more time staring at a laptop than usual.

And thanks to you for choosing this book out of the near-infinity of books out there. It means a lot.